And the angels whispered...

THE JOURNEY BACK TO
SPIRITUAL AWARENESS

Sarah B. Diamond

BALBOA.
PRESS
A DIVISION OF HAY HOUSE

Balboa Press books may be ordered through booksellers or by contacting:

Balboa Press
A Division of Hay House
1663 Liberty Drive
Bloomington, IN 47403
www.balboapress.com
1 (877) 407-4847

Because of the dynamic nature of the Internet, any web addresses or
links contained in this book may have changed since publication and
may no longer be valid. The views expressed in this work are solely those
of the author and do not necessarily reflect the views of the publisher,
and the publisher hereby disclaims any responsibility for them.

The author of this book does not dispense medical advice or prescribe the use
of any technique as a form of treatment for physical, emotional, or medical
problems without the advice of a physician, either directly or indirectly. The
intent of the author is only to offer information of a general nature to help
you in your quest for emotional and spiritual well-being. In the event you use
any of the information in this book for yourself, which is your constitutional
right, the author and the publisher assume no responsibility for your actions.

Any people depicted in stock imagery provided by Getty Images are
models, and such images are being used for illustrative purposes only.
Certain stock imagery © Getty Images.

Print information available on the last page.

ISBN: 978-1-9822-3505-5 (sc)
ISBN: 978-1-9822-3507-9 (hc)
ISBN: 978-1-9822-3506-2 (e)

Library of Congress Control Number: 2019950609

Balboa Press rev. date: 10/03/2019

Contents

The Encounter

◄o►

J UNE, 1995 LIFE CHANGED after my husband and I took separate vacations, and I started hearing voices in my head. Joe had ventured off to Las Vegas, NV to spend quality time with his two sons from a previous marriage, while I traveled to Chicago, IL to spend time with my family.

During my visit, I spent some time alone along Lake Michigan's shoreline as it was one of my favorite places to relax and unwind. It was also here I found myself face-to-face with an old love, a "true love." I had called Ray a few days prior to let him know I was going to be in town for a week. He then made arrangements to pick me up at my mother's apartment so we could go somewhere and talk.

Seeing Ray again had stirred up emotions in me I had not felt in years. The memories flooded back causing heartache even though years had passed since we had gone our separate ways. I had accepted a job transfer to San Diego, CA and, sometime later, Ray had decided to move away from Chicago too. Now, here we were, in the same place at the same time, sharing moments of our lives with one another. Yet, there were things about Ray I had already learned from my mother. Over the years, she would run into him when he had been in town on business. One thing, however, my mother chose not to share with me were Ray's messages asking me to call him. It wasn't until two weeks prior to my arriving in Chicago, after having run into Ray again, she gave me his message.

During my visit with Ray at the lake, I discovered he knew very little about my life in San Diego because he said all my mother would tell him was how happily married I was. Smiling, I too confirmed to him that was still the case. Unfortunately, Ray did not make the same statement to me about his marriage. He said he was not happy, but he stayed because of his children. Subconsciously, I wondered if he ever regretted not marrying me instead.

Deep down inside I was hoping he did. This unexpected revelation, however, had made me uncomfortable with my feelings. I felt if I continued to stay with Ray much longer, it would lead to more heartache. So, I chose to say goodbye instead. When I leaned forward to give him a farewell kiss, I looked up into his eyes and thought I saw sadness — or maybe it had been my reflection staring back at me. He drew me into his arms, kissed me slowly and tenderly until I responded passionately. It was then I knew I had never stopped loving him.

In less than an hour after Ray had picked me up, I was back at my mother's apartment. Depressed, I wanted to go for a drink so I invited my mother and sister, Faith, to join me. While sharing my feelings about Ray with them, I broke down and cried realizing I was now in love with two men.

A few days later I returned home to San Diego and to my husband. It was difficult for me to look at Joe without feeling guilty about how seeing Ray again had affected me so much. Knowing I could not keep these feelings to myself, I told Joe about the encounter and the emotional turmoil I was in. Joe, however, just wanted me to dismiss the incident just as he was willing to do. "Let's just go back to our lives the way we were." He said. But I couldn't.

Seeing Ray, and having to say goodbye to him once more, had been traumatic for me. I was experiencing depression and an emptiness I had never felt before. I couldn't understand what was wrong with me. After all, it had been almost 13 years since Ray and I had last seen each other. Now I found myself wanting him back in my life, and it appeared he wanted me back in his life too. He called. I called. Each time we expressed regrets about the past and tried to understand one another's feelings about the present. In doing so, however, we came to the realization that we both still had very strong feelings for one another. It was then we agreed not to talk to each other anymore. We had families to consider, and Ray and I knew we could never just be friends. After a month went by without a word, a voice in my head kept telling me to pick up the phone and call. I ignored this voice for over a week — then it yelled at me **"PICK UP THE PHONE!"** Contact - started the process all over again. I called. He called.

I needed help. I needed a psychic.

Past Life Experience

<o>

WHEN I WAS 18, my mother had introduced me to my first psychic, Crystal, who was well known in Chicago. There were those who believed in her psychic abilities and those who did not. I chose to believe. Over the years, her predictions for me had proved to be very accurate, except for one. She said Ray and I were going to get married and have two children. As I thought this was set in stone, I couldn't wait to tell Ray he was spoken for – it was predicted and therefore was going to happen. However, little did I know at the time he did have a say in the matter.

Ray said "No." After his first experience at wedded bliss ended in divorce, Ray assured me that he had no intention of getting married again anytime soon. Heartbroken, I went back to Crystal for a revised prediction. This time she foresaw me moving somewhere out West, and immediately I thought of Reno, NV where my aunt Liz lived. For years she had mentioned the idea of my moving there and now I was seriously considering it. However, before acting upon this current prediction of Crystal's, I decided to check into the possibility of a job transfer with the company I worked for. When I discovered there were no openings in the Reno office, I then made arrangements to visit my uncle Ken and his family in San Diego where I was able to set up an interview with another of the company's agencies. During my meeting, I was told there would be a position opening up in a couple of months, and I was offered the job if I wanted it. I set the wheels in motion to move to San Diego, and I was amazed at how everything fell into place so smoothly. Ray, on the other hand, thought I was overreacting by moving away, and that I was placing too much trust in what my "psychic" was telling me. Yet, I knew the time had come for me to move on. Our relationship wasn't going anywhere, and it hurt too much for me to continue seeing him. Sadly, our time together had come to an end, and I left Chicago without saying goodbye to him.

Living in San Diego, I continued to call Crystal on occasion for advice. I discontinued this practice shortly after Joe and I decided to get married. He too believed I was gullible and feared if my "psychic" were to predict a divorce for us, then that would be the end. To ease his mind, I promised Joe that I wouldn't look into the future anymore. Now, nearly 13 years later, that promise was going to be broken.

Never having sought a psychic or tarot reader in San Diego before, I started asking friends if they knew of anyone I could go to. Within days of my inquiry, Jan had made an appointment for me to see her "reader" whom she believed to be very accurate.

After my reading with Jackie, however, my impression had been somewhat different. If I had gone with my gut instinct, I would not have had her read for me in the first place just based on the atmosphere in this woman's home where my reading took place. From the onset, there were constant interruptions with dogs barking and her grandchildren running in and out of the house. In addition, there was a thunderstorm taking place outside that caused a huge tree branch to fall on the side of the house. It scared the heck out of both of us. Later I discovered Jackie had operated the tape recorder incorrectly by not switching the tape to Side B when Side A had finished. Instead she reloaded the tape again on Side A and taped over the first half of my reading. With all the distractions and no tape to refer to, I was unable to recall most of what Jackie had told me, except maybe I would be changing jobs in the near future. Nevertheless, I was very thankful for this bizarre experience; otherwise, I might not have met Angel.

Disappointed in Jan's "reader," I decided to find someone else to do another reading for me. This time I consulted the yellow pages. Based upon her location, which was across the street from my office, I selected Angel. From the moment I had met Angel at her office, I felt very comfortable and at ease. Within minutes I was confiding to her the confusion I was in regarding my feelings for my husband and another man. While Angel continued to listen as I talked, she laid tarot cards on the table which she used intuitively to help me with my dilemma.

One by one, Angel selected the cards that would reveal to her the past, present and future influences in my life that were affecting my current situation. After reflecting upon the cards that were laid out before her, Angel said they were the best she had seen in a long time for a client. However, she also said that the results of my reading would be based upon my own efforts to go within to find the answers I was looking for. According to Angel, "self" discovery was going to be crucial to my happiness. Only then, she stressed, would I make the right decisions. Angel also recommended I buy the book, **"Following Your Path,"** by Alexandra Collins Dickerman, and to start a journal immediately to record my thoughts.

Granted, everything Angel had said made sense to me, but I also needed some answers now where Ray was concerned. I told her no matter how hard I tried, I couldn't get him out of my thoughts. It was destructive to my marriage, and yet I couldn't stop myself from wanting to stay connected to him. Angel then advised me to undergo a past life experience.

Believing in reincarnation, Angel said we live many lifetimes. In each life we have a certain mission to accomplish with the help of our soul mates, not just one, but many, who travel through time with us. By looking into a past life, Angel thought this might shed some light as to the bonds I shared with Joe and Ray. Thus, willing to try almost anything, I scheduled an appointment for the following week.

THE PAST LIFE EXPERIENCE

Under hypnosis, Angel told me to enter an elevator and to stop it on any floor when I felt ready. When I got in, the elevator was pitch black and I started to cry. Everything was so dark for the longest time, and I kept telling her I felt so alone. Angel told me to stop the elevator and to step out to see if I could see anything. Still nothing. I got back in and it still seemed like a long time before I finally stopped and got off. Here, Angel told me to look at my feet and tell her what type of shoes I was wearing.

"Barefoot." I responded.

"What color are you?" Angel asked.

"Brown." I answered.

However, my vision had been somewhat blurred because I was walking through woods and it was still so very dark. Then in the distance I saw tribesmen dancing around a fire, but I was headed in another direction. Gradually, the scenery began to change and it was now daytime.

"What is your name?" Angel asked.

"Sarah." I replied.

My vision became clearer. I was a young white girl dressed in a long white dress walking toward a southern mansion. Angel wanted to know if I was going in the front door or back door. I told her I was going in the front door because it was my house. Entering, however, it felt very cold and empty. Angel told me to call out to my mother. I told her no one was there. I said they were all dead.

At this point, Angel said I would be going upstairs to where I would open three doors. Behind each door she wanted me to describe in detail to her what I saw.

First Door

Slowly I opened the door and looked inside. A cold chill ran down my back as I looked up and saw an Indian girl with long black braids hanging upside down. She was dead. Angel kept asking me who she was and who had killed her - I said I didn't know. This room scared me. I told Angel I was going to close the door now.

SECOND DOOR

A man was sitting at a desk writing. He turned around to see who had entered and just went back to what he was doing. He had white hair and was dressed in a gentleman's outfit. I said it was my father. Turning around, I walked out and closed the door.

THIRD DOOR

I hesitated. Angel told me it was OK. "Go ahead, Sarah. Open the door." There were two people in bed making love. I didn't know who the man was but said the woman was my mother. She started screaming at me to get out. I ran. I didn't even close the door.

I started skipping down the hallway. Angel asked me how old I was. "6," I replied. I ran down the stairs and outside to play. There was no one to play with. I was all alone.

Angel then wanted me to take her to the time when I attended my first party. Is it a birthday party or a coming out party?" She asked.

"No, it's just a party." I told her. As I headed downstairs to join the others, I mentioned to Angel how pretty I thought I looked in my beautiful new dress.

From the top of the staircase, I saw my mother below, up against the wall, with a drink in her hand, talking to a very handsome man. My father, on the other hand, was by himself on the opposite side of the room staring out a big bay window.

"Are there any boys here at the party you are interested in?" Angel asked.

Looking over the room, I responded, "No."

"In that case, Angel said, take me to the time Joe and Ray were in your life back then."

Once again, my vision changed and I saw the three of us standing around a horse carriage talking. Joe was dressed all in black and Ray all in white. We were friends.

"What was Ray's name in this life, Sarah?" Angel asked.

"Ben?" "Ben." I answered.

"And Joe's?" She asked.

"He's still Joe." I said.

"And which of the two do you want?" Angel asked.

"Ben." I replied.

"And why do you want Ben?" She asked.

Blushing, I confided in Angel that it was because of the way he looked at me. "Ben knows me, and he thinks I'm beautiful," I told her.

"And where's Joe," Angel continued.

"Gone," I said.

Once again Angel asked, "Gone where, Sarah?"

I told Angel repeatedly I didn't know where he was. She then asked me to find out from Ben where Joe went.

"Ben said he just left and he didn't know where he was going," I answered.

"Ok, Sarah." Angel said. "I want you to go back to when it was just you and Joe talking."

"He's yelling at me." I told her.

"Why," asked Angel.

"Because I wouldn't go away with him." I answered.

"Why wouldn't you go with him, Sarah?" She asked.

Knowingly, I answered. "Because Joe just wants me for my money."

I told Angel that when I looked at Ben, he was my light; everything was bright; he was my life. After hearing that, Angel chose to bring closure to my past life experience. "Ok, Sarah, I now want you to take me to the time when you die. How old are you," She asked.

"84." I whispered.

Angel said reassuringly, "You will not be afraid because the angels will come and take you into the light. Are you ready to die, Sarah?"

"Yes." I answered.

Within seconds, total blackness had come over me. All of a sudden flashes of light were bringing me up — what an absolutely beautiful feeling. And as I was ascending, Angel asked me, "What are the angels telling you to do?"

"Go to Ray. He's my light." I responded.

Then, Angel's last question. "And what would you ask of the angels?"

Crying, I answered. "To watch over Joe."

Sarah

<o>

T HE HARDEST THING ABOUT writing a self-discovery book is having to reflect on the type of person I WAS. Hopefully, forgiveness is in the hearts of those I had hurt – that was then and this is now. Maybe they would like the "new" me. I do.

Not wanting to appear egotistical, however, I grew up believing I was pretty and smart because that's what others told me. Sometimes another's remark would cause me to become a little conceited, especially, when at the age of 13, a male friend of my parents told me that if I had brains to go along with my beauty I would be dangerous. Even then, men flirted with me, but being young and naive, I didn't take any of their advances seriously.

I was interested in boys my own age, and if another girl liked the same one I did, it would become a contest to sec which one of us would get him. However, once the challenge was over, I then lost interest in the boy. This had set the pattern for my teens and adult life — competing to see if I was prettier or smarter. Winning was the important thing; not the prize.

I also learned early in life not to dwell on the negative if things did not turn out the way I wanted, especially where men were concerned. As a romantic, I was always falling in love. While some relationships had been very endearing, the infatuations eventually wore off and I ended up finding someone new.

Thus, when Ray had entered my life, I thought it was going to be just another temporary fling.

Ray And Sarah

◄○►

MY MOST PRECIOUS MEMORY of Ray is that of our first kiss, and every one of his kisses after that still had the same effect on me. Whenever our lips and bodies touched, I felt myself being completely absorbed into his very being until we had become one.

This man had affected me like no other. From the first time I had laid eyes on him, there had been a knowingness within me he was my true love. From the very beginning, I felt he loved me too. For months after we had started seeing each other, I waited for Ray to say he loved me. When he didn't, I said it first expecting him to reciprocate, but no such luck. Still, believing that it was just a matter of time before he would say those three words I longed to hear, I continued to wait.

After a year of an on-again, off-again relationship, my resolve had diminished, and I no longer believed there was a future for us. It had become obvious to me that I had been kidding myself all along into thinking there had been more to our relationship than just the physical attraction. Believing that to be the case, it hurt too much for me to continue seeing him so I moved away.

Yet, one month later Ray was in San Diego asking me if I was ready to come back. "To what?" I asked. "The way things were?" Ray did not make a commitment, but now there was hope. He finally said he loved me.

We continued our relationship for another five years long distance. Without a commitment still, I decided to call it quits. Resorting to a lie so Ray would let me go once and for all, I told him I was getting married. Funny, he said he was getting married too, but he wasn't lying.

Joe And Sarah

—◄○►—

A T THE AGE OF 29, I was ready for commitment and a serious relationship. Two months before my final goodbye to Ray, I joined a private singles club in hopes of meeting that "special" someone.

Shortly thereafter, my prayers were answered, and that someone had entered my life. With his dark good looks and easy going manner, I fell in love with Joe and married him a year later.

With marriage came motherhood, except it would be on a part-time basis only. Joe's two sons from a previous marriage lived with their mother some distance away. Occasionally, the boys would come to stay with us for periods at a time. Thus, I had mainly watched them grow from afar to when they would eventually have families of their own.

Moreover, my marriage had brought me contentment. Joe and I were truly happy, and we rarely ever argued. For the most part we were able to resolve any problems we faced by working together. Hence, when Ray reappeared back in my life, I didn't hesitate going to Joe and telling him about the emotional turmoil I was experiencing.

This time, however, Joe couldn't help. I needed someone else. I needed God.

The Missing Link

◄○►

G ROWING UP CATHOLIC, L was taught to believe in certain concepts, but even as a child, I was unable to accept all of them to be true. Still, I was grateful for my religious upbringing as it had instilled in me the need to stay connected to God.

As I thought about my connection to Him and my earlier years, it brought back a memory of a dream I had when I was 19:

High upon a mountain top, I was taken to a castle where I was told I was going to be offered wealth beyond my wildest dreams. I was led to an empty room with only a large treasure chest positioned in the middle of the floor. Overflowing with jewels and gold, I was told they were mine to keep. Then, from out of nowhere, a photographer appeared to take my picture outside. Exiting from two large French doors opening out to unbelievable scenery, I left the room to join him. Once I stepped outdoors, everything had disappeared, and I found myself all alone at the bottom of the hill. Within moments, I saw people dressed in white coming down the mountain to join me, and a very serene feeling had come over me. There was one man in particular who had stood out from the crowd, and the closer he got to me, I realized it was Christ. He took my hand and asked me to follow Him. Later my dream revealed it was just a play with actors playing a role. Afterwards I awoke in a cold sweat unable to move the arm Christ had touched. I told my mom about my dream and she thought it could have been a sign for me to become a nun.

Now, many years later, my Catholic upbringing was resurfacing, and I wanted to start going back to church. Moreover, I wanted my husband with me. Joe, on the other hand, did not want to go, and I would end up going alone.

Returning to church had proved to be very emotional for me. There were many times during the services where tears would come, and I would have to fight to maintain control. Solace would eventually come from the messages I had received from the Sunday sermons. There was one in particular that had touched me deeply when the priest said, "God answers all of our questions in time, and when we need them the most. We as humans are very impatient and want to be able to understand things as they happen."

After much reflection, I realized slowly but surely the answers were indeed coming. Soon, I was able to start seeing very clearly the lessons I needed to learn.

Then there was another message I had taken to heart when the priest had said, "Once we find our way back to God, our lives will never be the same."

Mine was never the same again.

A New Direction

◄o►

I HAD TAKEN ANGEL'S ADVICE and started keeping a journal.
Writing enabled me to express on paper what I was afraid to
express verbally to Ray and Joe. Also, by writing my thoughts
and prayers down, it helped me to put things into perspective. I
began to look at my relationships with Ray and Joe in a new light.
My feelings for Ray had led me to question my marriage and the
direction I was headed. I found myself asking if I had settled for less
than "true love" when I married Joe.

Admitting the answer to myself was one thing; admitting it
Joe was something else. Later I would discover he had suspected
the truth before I did, and it would lead back to the first night we
met when he asked me why I moved to San Diego. "Broken heart,"
I told him. I had no idea at the time how true that statement was.
Honestly, when I married Joe, I believed I loved him with all my
heart — and I did — but the heart had been defective.

It appeared old wounds had not yet healed, and it tormented me to know I still loved Ray. Angel's counsel was helping, but knowing how Ray and Joe felt about my delving into the unknown, I kept my visits with her from both of them. A lot of my decisions had been from her input — the journal, reading the book **"Following Your Path,"** and meditating. But after hearing the angel message towards the end of my past life experience, "Go to Ray. He's my light," I found myself asking Joe for a divorce so I could move back to Chicago to be closer to Ray.

Joe had remained calm during my request. Instead, he questioned my state of mind. "Are you crazy?" he asked. Yes, he understood it was possible to still be in love with someone else, but he also said there was no future in it. Nonetheless, I still felt the need to go back to Chicago.

"There's no need for you to rush into anything." Joe said. "You've been under a lot of pressure lately at work. Take some time off and go for a visit. Just don't do anything drastic."

I agreed. Besides, I decided to call Ray to find out how he felt about my getting a divorce and moving back to Chicago to where I could be with my family again and be closer to him too since he lived just a couple hours away. At first, his reaction had been encouraging in that he said he was looking forward to the prospect of my return. Later, after having a few days to think about it, he had become apprehensive. Consequently, the day before I was to fly out of San Diego, Ray had called to tell me that even though he was disillusioned with his marriage one factor remained constant, his love for his children. Ray said he could never do anything to jeopardize their welfare, so he had asked me not to come.

I went anyway. Just because Ray didn't want to see me, I still needed time with my family. So in mid-October, just four months after the "encounter," I was on a flight back to Chicago. Fortunately, before leaving San Diego, I had asked Joe to forgive me and to let him know I no longer wanted a divorce. With the assurance that I would not see Ray again, Joe felt confident that our marriage could resume back to normal. He forgave me and chose to blame my actions on mid-life crisis, stress from my job, and even the diet pills I had been taking which Joe thought could possibly be affecting my brain.

I kept my promise to Joe and did not see Ray while I was in Chicago. When I returned home to San Diego, neither one of us brought the subject up. However, even though Joe had been understanding and forgiving, a gap now existed between us. There were doubts.

The uncertainty continued when Ray called me two weeks later to apologize for his reaction to my coming to Chicago. He said he had strong feelings for me, and he didn't know how to handle them. Obviously, I could relate; I was having the same problem too.

Over the past several months after the "encounter," our phone conversations had us both wondering what direction we were headed. We reminisced about feelings, passion, and what went wrong. It had been a time of enlightenment for both of us. By communicating now, something that we did very little of back then, we realized how strong our feelings were for one another. This in turn led us to discover that neither one of us had ever stopped loving the other. Once this realization hit home, however, guilt overcame both of us, and we decided it was best not to talk to each other anymore. The truth had not only hurt us; it would hurt other people too.

Trying to let go was easier said than done. My need to stay connected to Ray was more powerful. He was in my thoughts every moment and being close to him was all I could think of. Then there was the angel message, "Go to Ray. He's my light." Hence, the solution seemed clear to me; get a divorce and move back to Chicago. To Ray, however, he saw it as a problem - not a solution - and that's when he had asked me not to come.

Now, two weeks later, he was telling me he regretted not seeing me while I was in Chicago. I told Ray I was no longer getting a divorce, and he sounded relieved. I also told him my husband had been understanding and forgiving and that everything seemed to be getting back to normal.

But it wasn't getting back to normal. Over the next two months, Joe and I were growing apart, and every day I would write in my journal asking God for guidance. I then thought if Joe and I started going back to church it would help bring us closer together, but I ended up going alone.

Thus the gap between Joe and I continued to grow. My commitment to him and to our marriage was no longer 100%. The word divorce came up again. This time Joe exploded. "How could seeing this guy once in June come between us?" He demanded. "Has our whole marriage been a lie?" He asked furiously. Then the most hurtful question of all: "Did you marry me on the rebound?"

It's as if he threw cold water in my face and brought me out of a trance. The thought of marrying Joe on the rebound had never occurred to me. Was it possible? I reflected back on my journal. Yes. It was possible.

Step by step, as if my journal were in front of me, I tried to explain to Joe why I no longer wanted to be his wife. Even though I didn't want to hurt him further, I told him the truth because it was the only thing that made sense.

I sat on the couch with my head down and cried while relaying parts of my journal to him; my feelings for Ray and for him; trying to find the answers through tarot readers, then going back to church and how I wanted him to be a part of that. I did not look up once as I told him about the past life experience, and how I believed there was a force trying to bring Ray and I together. Joe never interrupted; he just listened until I finished. Then, unexpectedly, his response shocked me. He blamed himself for not realizing how important going back to church had become to me or to our marriage.

Determined, however, to have our marriage work, Joe asked me to go to a marriage counselor with him. I agreed to go even though I knew the outcome was going to be the same. After our one and only session with the counselor the following week, Joe realized it too. Reluctantly, he said he would abide by my wishes but asked that I wait until after the upcoming holidays before proceeding with my plans.

Without confiding in anyone that we were getting a divorce, Joe and I continued to party with friends and family as if nothing were wrong. We also went to a Christmas church event that featured a fabulous choir. Many of the songs they sang had to do with seeing the "light," but the words to one song in particular, "Coming Out

Of The Darkness," caused tears to stream down my face. When Joe noticed, he put his arm around me and drew me closer to him. I couldn't help but love this man. So why wasn't that enough to stay married to him?

Because no matter how hard I tried to dismiss it, there was still something else missing in my life. There remained a void in my heart that Joe's love could not fill. For a brief moment in time, being with Ray again had rekindled a feeling so long ago forgotten — a different kind of love. It's impossible for me to try and explain the difference between my love for Joe and my love for Ray. It's like asking a mother to explain the love she feels for one child versus another, or the love she feels for her husband versus the love she feels for her children. There are various degrees of love, some immeasurable and some unexplainable. Fortunately for me, Joe did not ask me to explain. He said he would continue to love me, just as I said I would continue to love him.

With that understanding, Joe and I were able to talk openly about the divorce with each other. We discussed our financial situation and decided to refinance the mortgage on the house in order to use some of the equity to pay off debts and split the remaining proceeds to give each of us a cushion for starting our new lives.

I then made arrangements to fly back to Chicago to break the news to my family and to see Ray. I had called him the week before I was to arrive in town to tell him of my plans to get a divorce and possibly moving back. This time he did want to see me, and he asked me to call him on his cell phone after my flight arrived to set up a time and place to meet for dinner.

Before seeing Ray though, I wanted clarification on the angel message that had been haunting me ever since my past life experience, "Go to Ray. He's my light." I met with Angel the day before my trip to Chicago, and she told me things I did not want to hear.

"The message was for closure, Sarah." Angel said. "In order to move forward, you need to let go of the past." Unfortunately, I had not anticipated this kind of interpretation from her nor was I happy with the rest of her predictions either. She told me that Ray and his wife were getting along better now, and she felt my presence in his life might jeopardize any chance they would have of working things out.

After hearing this, I started to cry. I wanted to believe Ray still loved me as much as I loved him. I wanted to believe that someday he would get a divorce because he was so unhappy in his present situation. I did not want to believe anything that Angel was now telling me. I was angry with her, and I was angry with God for having brought him back into my life. I did not want to have to say goodbye to Ray again. I was crying uncontrollably now. Even Angel was getting caught up in my hysterics. I had her in tears too. "Are you sure it was for closure?" I sobbed.

To pacify me, Angel gave me an exercise to do before I was to see Ray the next day. "Go home and meditate." she said. "Ask the angels, if Ray is meant to be, let him stay; if not, let him go. Ask the angels for some kind of sign, and you will have your answer when you see him tomorrow."

I did as she asked and somewhere in midair flying back to Chicago, it hit me that the sign would be in his kiss.

Ray and I met when I was 22. We worked for separate companies on the same floor of a bank building located in downtown Chicago. After hearing he had moved into my apartment building, I invited him over for a drink. A few days later, he called and invited me over to his place and, even though I had a tension headache, I went. Minutes after arriving at Ray's, my headache grew worse. I mentioned to him the discomfort I was in and asked if he would massage my neck. He obliged. Gently at first, his touch had felt very soothing then very sensual. Pausing to look deeply into my eyes, Ray then proceeded to cover my lips with his. Slowly and deliberately, he kissed me tenderly until my mouth responded passionately. The more intense our kisses became, the more lightheaded I felt. I was on cloud nine and my headache was gone. I was in love once again.

Now, back in Chicago and just minutes before seeing Ray again, I wondered what his kiss would tell me. Shortly thereafter, I had my answer as soon as our lips touched and the angels whispered "let him go."

Intuition Workshop

O N THE FLIGHT BACK to Chicago, even before knowing what the outcome was going to be, I started to prepare myself mentally to let Ray go just in case what Angel had told me had been true. To be sure, I waited until he kissed me to see if things had changed between us. Instantly, the moment he pressed his lips to mine, I knew they had. Still, needing more confirmation, I came right out and asked Ray, "Are you and your wife getting along better?"

"Yes," he said. "It was touch and go there for a while, but things are better now."

Silently within, I heard the words again to let him go. Without Ray, I had no desire to move back to Chicago. I never told him about the tarot readings, past life experience or angel exercise I had done to determine my future. Emotionally lost, I then called Angel from my mother's apartment a few days later to let her know what had transpired between Ray and I. Once again, I found myself asking her for guidance. "Should I go back to Joe?" I wondered. He was calling me almost every day to see what my future plans were. "No, I wasn't moving back to Chicago." I told him. "And, yes, I realized there was no future for Ray and I." Yet, I still didn't know where that left us. Angel then suggested I do the same exercise for Joe that I had done for Ray. Once again I asked the angels to give me a sign if Joe was "meant to be."

However, when Joe picked me up at the San Diego airport a few days later, I had no sign or answer – I just had too many doubts.

The next day I went to Angel for what would turn out to be my last reading with her. Reflecting back on Angel's final words to me as I was leaving her office, I suspected months later that she knew this was going to be our last meeting together. "I hope you have a sense of humor." She said. "You're going to need it." Those statements, along with the rest of her predictions, including a job change, had sounded pretty ominous at the time. However, according to Angel, if I could face certain fears and let go of the past, then I would be able to find true love once again.

It was this prediction I wanted to believe most of all. Yet, considering all the heartache I had been through lately, I wondered if it really was worth all the pain to try and find that elusive dream called "true love" just because Angel had told me it was possible.

For me the answer was "yes." More than anything else in this world I wanted to be able to experience that special kind of love again.

However, not knowing if Joe and I could work things out and possibly find that love together, I held off filing for a divorce. With the decision to separate instead, I signed a six month lease on an apartment located not too far from our home that would become available the middle of March. Even though I was anxious to move into my own place as soon as possible, I realized this timeframe actually worked out better for Joe and I as the refinancing on the house was scheduled to close the end of February. The funds from this would provide each of us with a cushion to start new lives just in case our arrangement became permanent because sometimes, no matter how much we want things to work out, they just don't.

I came to terms with that concept when Ray called shortly after my return from Chicago. In my mind I had let him go, but not in my heart. Finally, I just gave up the struggle of trying to say goodbye to him once and for all and allowed him to remain a part of my life. After telling Ray about the separation, I agreed to stay in touch with him by phone once or twice a month.

Comfortable with my new arrangements with Joe and Ray, I then went back to my program of self-discovery which Angel had stressed was going to be crucial to my happiness. I continued to write in my journal, read and meditate. Yet, I felt there was still something else I needed to be doing. Soon after reading the book, **"Following Your Path,"** I discovered what it was. I needed to develop and listen to my inner voice – intuition.

What a coincidence. My friend Ann recently asked me to attend an intuition workshop with her that was going to begin in a couple of weeks. Little did I know, by taking this course, it would lead me on a journey into the unknown that would change my life forever. However, months later I realized this journey had actually been evolving over a long period of time. The sequence of events which had led me to this point in my life were not by accident; they were all a part of my "spiritual" awakening.

A little over a year ago, I had introduced myself to Ann who worked for a different company on the same floor I did. Three years of seeing her almost every day but not knowing her by name, I decided it was time to introduce myself to her. This in turn led me to start introducing myself to the other women on the floor whom I did not know. Then, I decided not to stop there. With the holidays fast approaching, I thought it would be nice to organize a Christmas party to where everyone could meet each other. I discussed my idea with the owners of the firm where I was now employed as an office manager. With their approval, I set about to plan a "5th floor" Christmas party. Beginning with all the secretaries and other office managers, I sought their help in getting their companies to participate. Then, after having obtained everyone's cooperation, we planned a pot luck, along with each office agreeing to donate a gift to be drawn as a door prize. Next, in order to hold the party in the 5th floor lobby, I needed to obtain approval from the property management company located on the first floor. At first they said "No" because they thought it might be disruptive to some of the tenants. However, since I was able to assure them that we had 100% cooperation from all the 5th floor offices, they finally agreed. Thus, in appreciation, we invited their office staff too.

The party had been a total success except for one thing, I almost missed it. Just a few days prior, I had fallen down some stairs at home and severely sprained my ankle. The doctor told me to stay off my feet for a week, but with the use of crutches and my husband's assistance, I was able to attend. However, it was because of this accident that I decided to start taking diet pills. The extra weight I was carrying around while hobbling on crutches took its toll on me.

Following the Christmas party, my acquaintance with Ann grew when a group of us women from the 5th floor offices decided to start meeting once a month for lunch. In addition to having obtained permission from each of our employers for these get-togethers, they were also kind enough to extend our lunch hours.

Nine months after having initiated these luncheons, I found myself sharing the story of my past life experience with the girls. Afterwards, Ann had expressed an interest in having it done, so I then recommended Angel to her. In return, Ann chose to reveal a secret to me that I had found very interesting.

Confessing that she had been studying the ancient art of Tarot herself for some time, Ann had also surprised me when she had told me that anyone could learn. Fascinated, I then asked her if she would do a reading for me, and she agreed. A few nights later when Joe had to work late, I provided the dinner and Ann provided the cards. From the moment Ann had placed the first card on the table, I was hooked and wanted to learn this ancient art myself. The next day after my reading, I ordered my first deck of cards through my book club after I had seen them on sale in my recent month's flyer. Being naive on the subject, however, I didn't realize tarot cards were also available at some local book stores.

Thus, this was the sequence of events which led to my attending an intuition workshop with Ann who then in turn introduced me to Dee.

Dee, a professional intuitive counselor, had been persuaded

by several of her clients, Ann among them, to conduct such a workshop. Scheduled as a six-week course on Wednesday nights, Ann and I attended Dee's first class along with four other women. Instantly, all of us bonded, and we spent the majority of the evening getting to know one another instead of talking about intuition. Dee did, however, recommend several books for reading on the subject, and she had lent me her copy of "Living in the Light," by Shakti Gawain. I had promised to return it to her the following week when she and I were scheduled to meet alone. Since Ann had recommended her so highly, I had made an appointment with Dee for a reading.

A Reading By Dee

S OMEWHERE BACK IN TIME I had met Paul, an officer in the
United States Air Force, who was dating Linda, a friend of
my mother. Paul was also the first person to introduce me to the
ancient art of Tarot.

Discussing Crystal one day with Linda and Paul, the topic of
Tarot had also come up when Paul had mentioned that he too could
see into the future with the use of these special cards. Believing it
was possible for some people to see into the future, I found it hard
to believe using a deck of cards could do the same thing. Still, I
was intrigued that a man of Paul's stature was delving into the
unknown this way, so I allowed him to give me a demonstration.
The outcome of my reading, however, was that I chose to believe in
Crystal's predictions over that of a deck of cards. In time, however,
I have come to believe in both, especially after meeting Angel
who had used her psychic abilities, along with tarot cards, in
counseling me.

Following up on Ann's recommendation, I found myself back in Dee's apartment anxiously awaiting to have her "read" for me, plus I also wanted to compare Dee's abilities to Angel's.

While Dee was getting the cards and tape recorder ready, I was perusing her varied collection of tarot cards.

"These decks, do they mean anything specifically to you?" I asked her.

"Each one means different things to me intuitively." She said.

Shuffling, Dee was putting her energy onto the cards and, while doing so, one of them had popped out of the deck. "Oh, interesting," She said. "The wish card."

Then, wanting my energy on the cards too, Dee handed me the deck to shuffle. When I had finished, she had me cut them three ways. Next, she took the deck and started placing the cards into what is known as a "spread" on the table. Then, she began my reading.

The first topic that we discussed was my upcoming separation from Joe in which Dee saw me definitely moving, around March 15th she thought. According to Dee, it was important that I make this change in my life because she felt there was something I needed to do, and if I wasn't careful, I would talk myself out of it. The move, she said, would be good not just for me, but for Joe too, in that each of us would be able to discover a lot about ourselves.

"Are you thinking about taking classes?" She then asked.

"Just with you so far." I told her.

"I do see you taking more classes though. Maybe that's what I'm picking up. Maybe this class is a start." She said.

Talking briefly about the intuition workshop, Dee and I felt this course was going to be a lot of fun if the first session had been any indication as to how well all of us women were going to get along. Inexplicably, it appeared there was a strong connection between all us who were taking the class.

"Are you looking for another job?" She interjected.

Once again I was reminded of Jackie's and Angel's predictions that they too had seen a job change for me. "You know I've had two other people tell me that." I told Dee. "That totally amazes me."

"And it's going to be sudden too." Dee said. "There are a lot of changes coming up for you."

Excited by this prospect, I told Dee I was looking forward to change and to whatever the future had in store for me. Then Dee touched on a subject close to my heart.

"A male from your past is going to come up." She said. "Or you're going to run into somebody or something is going to happen. It's another issue you will resolve. It's something that's going to tell you about yourself and you'll be real happy about it."

Confessing my love for another man, I proceeded to tell Dee the story about Ray and how I had been carrying a torch for him for over the last 20 years. "I finally accepted the fact that I still love him." I told her. "He just called me yesterday wanting to know how everything was going. He'll always stay a part of my life. And as long as I can talk to him, that's all I want. Like you said, it was a very happy resolution."

Then Dee went on to predict pretty much of what Angel had told me earlier too — "true love" was a definite possibility.

Sooner than that, Dee predicted I would be taking a trip with a girlfriend around the end of April or the first part of May. Thus far, however, I had not made any such plans.

"Sounds like my months are going to get real active." I said to Dee. "And everything you have told me in my reading has just reiterated some of the same things that my others readers, Jackie and Angel had told me earlier."

Dee responded, "That's what I try to tell people. It should validate sort of what you already feel — "yeah, I've felt that" or "I knew that was going to happen"... Because our job is to let people know that their dreams can come true and to follow their own feelings."

The Partnership

-◄o►-

AFTER MY READING WITH Dee, I felt exhilarated. I was looking forward to change. The date of my upcoming move into my apartment had now been confirmed for the middle of March, and maybe, if my "readers" were correct, I would be changing jobs too in the near future. Moreover, I wondered about the possibility of finding true love once again — only time would tell.

Until then, I decided to delve further into the unknown by becoming more familiar with metaphysics through such authors as Deepak Chopra, Shakti Gawain, Louise Hay and Stuart Wilde. Their philosophies on universal law, intuition, visualization and meditation inspired me to view life differently. As a result, by altering my thinking, my whole world changed.

However, it was **"The Celestine Prophecy,"** by James Redfield, that touched my very soul. One by one, nine insights were revealed in this book and, by accepting each of them to be true, I exchanged old beliefs for new which were helping me to become more spiritually enlightened. From the first insight, I had begun to understand the importance of coincidences and events in my life and the the influences they were having on the progression of my spiritual journey. Thus, the significance of the next event had become quite apparent to me later on when the time would come for me to comprehend some of the other insights.

On March 9, 1996, my tarot cards arrived from the book club. I was now ready to learn about the ancient art of Tarot, where it originated from, and how it worked. Yet, according to the book, no one has ever been able to answer those questions.

For centuries Tarot has continued to exist because of a belief system that this ancient art is able to provide insight into one's life. Willing to test this theory out for myself, I sat down at the dining room table and prepared to do my first, very own tarot reading.

Following the instructions in the book, I shuffled the cards while I silently asked my Higher Power (God) for guidance. Then, when I felt it was time to stop shuffling, I laid ten cards out in what was referred to as the Celtic Cross Spread and then I read what each card represented.

The first card I drew, which was to reflect the situation I found myself in at the present moment (moving), was the **Ace of Wands**: New Beginning.

The second position described what was generating conflict or stirring up matters in the situation, and the card I drew was the **Three of Wands:** Soul mates, Partnership

The **Four of Swords** card was drawn in the third position which represented the atmosphere hanging over the immediate situation: Need to meditate

Then the message given in the next card drawn had brought tears to my eyes as the truth continued to hurt.

The **Three of Swords**, drawn in the fourth position, reflected what was really behind the apparent surface situation: Separation

Position five described what was behind my present situation. **The Hermit**: Aloneness

And according to the **Strength** card I had drawn for position six, it was to represent what was forthcoming: Courage

Then the **Temperance** card I had drawn for position seven was to reflect my attitude in the situation: Develop a balanced heart

Position eight described the image which those around us - friends and family – hold of our situation and ourselves. The card drawn was **Justice**: Reaping what you sow; Potential legal dealings

Position nine represented one's hopes and fears which can be described by one card, for all the cards in the Tarot deck have a double face. And the card I had drawn was **The Chariot**: Direction, where to go

And last but not least, the outcome of my situation, **The Lovers** card: Choices of the heart

My own reading had proved to be very accurate and helpful. The tarot cards had provided me with insight as to what I was feeling and why. Plus, they also helped confirm the need for me to be alone at this time. However, the final outcome card of the Lovers puzzled me. I didn't think there was any choice to be made between Ray or Joe. And there wasn't. Another love was about to enter my life, a new partnership.

Just two weeks after moving into my apartment, I found myself making a major career decision. Suddenly, the job change that all the "readers" had predicted was about to come to fruition.

One night as Ann and I were preparing to leave our intuition class, Dee casually mentioned to us that a friend of hers was advising her to look for investors to sponsor her workshops. After some discussion, Ann and I thought this would be a great business venture, and we ended up proposing a partnership to Dee instead.

However, Dee was uncomfortable with the idea of partners at first because she was not business oriented, and she told us that the only reason she was looking for investors now was to be able to obtain capital to meet her monthly expenditures while expanding her workshops. However, once Ann and I assured her that we could handle everything, including her financial obligations until the workshops started making money, she agreed. Hence began the foundation of our partnership.

The time had been right for both Ann and I to make a career change. Ann's position at her firm was being eliminated the end of April anyway due to a company merger, and I now had some extra money in my bank account from the refinancing on the house. In addition to my taking a chance on a new career, I also decided to get a divorce.

"What's wrong with just a separation for now?" Joe asked. "Why divorce?"

Several reasons came to mind. The new business venture — quitting a good job and investing money in a partnership that could be risky — I did not want to be accountable to Joe regarding these decisions. Plus, with a separation, I felt we were both putting our lives on hold just waiting to see what the other one was going to do. I wanted to be able to venture out into the unknown without restrictions or limitations. Most importantly though that special something was still missing.

"It doesn't mean we have to stop loving each other," I said. "It's just not fair for either one of us to put our lives on hold waiting to see what the other one does."

Joe conceded. We filed for divorce.

Sedona, AZ

─◄o►─

G OING AT SUCH A fast pace and changing practically everything in my life, I was now ready for a vacation.

"How about the three of us taking a trip somewhere to celebrate our partnership?" I suggested to Ann and Dee. "Besides, it would also be nice to see how we travel together if we are going to do workshops nationwide."

In agreement, Ann and Dee suggested Sedona, Arizona which they both believed to be a very spiritual place. As I was unfamiliar with this location, they informed me it was considered a metaphysical haven where people could discuss their beliefs openly with others, along with speculating about UFO activity in the area. There were also vortexes they wanted to visit where people have claimed to receive "messages" from beyond.

Agreeing to the location, Ann, Dee and I prepared a "wish list" of things we wanted on our trip by following Stuart Wilde's advice from his book, "Miracles:" Accordingly, we wrote down everything we wanted believing that our wishes would come true.

In my journal I recorded the following "wish" list for our Sedona trip:

May 1 - May 8, 1996

. Leave 5 a.m. - beautiful day for our drive.

. Safe travel, dependable car (comfortable) - good weather and good roads, and no detours the entire trip.

. Hotel accommodations be everything that we desire, and more, at very reasonable rates.

. A townhome for our entire stay in Sedona

- 3 bedrooms and 3 bathrooms

- Kitchen and fireplace

- Right on the water with no bugs

- Very modern accommodations

- Lots of people around but very quiet at night.

. May the condo fall into our laps at a fantastic rate. May it also have a beautiful landscape.

Dee sees patio. Large rooms for each of us to find solace when we need it. This will be a very safe and secure place for us to stay. Please provide VCR also. Two-story townhome preferably.

. Peace, knowledge, wisdom, understanding of each other, solidification of our unity, and lots and lots of fun and laughter.

. All three of us very energized and in tuned to each other's needs.

. Safe travel going and coming back - nothing but pleasant experiences along the way.

. Show us the way to begin our joint venture where everything will come to us easily in setting things up.

With our wish list in hand, we were ready to begin our trip. However, before we even got started, we found ourselves compromising on our "wish list," beginning with the time of departure. Having forewarned Ann and I that she was not a morning person, Dee had requested an extra 1/2 hour to get ready. With no other time constraints, we loaded up my car and headed out on a beautiful Wednesday morning.

We arrived in Sedona around 2:00 p.m., and because we believed tourist season was over, we did not make any reservations ahead of time. Moreover, though, we believed the Universe would see to our needs based on the "wish" list we had composed earlier. With our written list in hand, we were ready to find accommodations — first stop, the Tourist Information Center. Here we picked up a few brochures, read the descriptions, and selected an inn that was located close to Main Street and within walking distance to the stores and restaurants.

Walking into the "office," I told the gentleman seated at a computer I had a "wish" list for accommodations while staying in Sedona. "Any chance you can comply with some of the things on our list?" I asked him. Mike, the owner, laughed and said he thought we might have a hard time finding a place to stay for the week let alone finding one that could comply with our "wish" list. According to Mike, almost everything was booked, "high tourist season," he said. Still, he did have two rooms available for two nights if we wanted them. I hesitated. Mike then went one step further by calling some of his friends who owned hotels and resorts in the area to see if they had anything available - nothing. So we booked for the two nights he had and decided to look later for another place to stay. However, we didn't have to look any further. Mike did it all for us. He was persistent. He knew someone who handled rental properties - condos and townhomes (honest to God). Needless to say, the remainder of our stay was spent in an immaculate two-story townhome that had almost everything on our list - except it wasn't on the water; it was on a golf course.

Once again the Universe continued to send us other messages through visualization and symbolism. Seeing all three of our names written in the clouds was very impressive, and for some reason I was now having reoccurring dreams that I had as a child featuring the mythical horse Pegasus. Yet, it was the "voices" at the vortexes I would continue to hear for a long time. There are several energy currents known as vortexes in Sedona where people have claimed to receive "messages" from beyond. Inexplicably, at the three vortexes we visited, I too received messages.

Mike had given us the names and locations of the vortexes he thought we might be interested in going to, beginning with the one known as Cathedral Rock. Here, we followed a path to a stream where each of us chose a place to meditate. Dee sat on a rock a few feet above me while I sat with my feet dangling in the water, and Ann was some distance to our right walking around. All was quiet, very peaceful. Then, in the silence, I heard a voice inside my head repeating the word "write." That was all I kept hearing, just that one word. But what was I to write about – the partnership – I pondered this thought for another five minutes when all of a sudden I felt this need to leave. Exactly at that moment, Dee stood up and Ann started walking towards us. Without a word, we knew it was time to go.

The following day we visited our next vortex, Bell Rock. This time, however, Ann, Dee and I decided to spread out a little farther apart from each other, with me choosing to sit at the base of the rock. For fifteen minutes I had sat there without "hearing" anything, but then out of the blue came the voice within that said "Mike will help." Immediately, I thought of Mike at the inn and wondered if he had a message for me. For a few more minutes as I sat there debating whether or not to get up, I looked down at the ground and saw an object that caught my eye. There was a small piece of wood lying next to my shoe which I felt compelled to reach down and pick it up. Turning it sideways, I held it next to the ring on my finger and realized it closely resembled the outline of my custom-made ring. With keepsake in hand to remind me of this moment, I thanked the Universe for my messages and went to join Ann and Dee who knew too, without a word, that it was time for us to leave.

Arriving back at the inn, we saw Mike sitting alone in the courtyard. We walked over to thank him for his help in directing us to the vortexes and proceeded to engage him in conversation about intuition, tarot readings and dreams. Being an open-minded person himself, Mike told us about his wife's dreams being prophetic and over the years he had learned to heed their messages. Plus, he said that she kept a journal by her bed to record them as soon as she woke up, and it was then I had silently thanked Mike for giving me my message.

In my 20's I had realized too how powerful my dreams were. They provided me with solutions to problems I encountered, and sometimes they would reveal glimpses into my future. Unfortunately, as I grew older, my dreams had become less memorable and they started to subside. I missed the stories they had to tell and of what was to come. Mike's stories about his wife's prophetic dreams had reminded me of my own, and while he talked, I was also getting a subliminal message that my dreams and visions were going to return soon and to record them.

With just two days left in Sedona, Ann, Dee and I decided to visit one more vortex near Boyton Canyon. Here, we followed along a trail until we came across a clearing where we decided to stop and meditate. Five minutes later the three of us were ready to leave. I had received my message, "Believe."

Going Home

◄○►

AFTER HAVING RECEIVED MY tarot cards that fateful day in March, I had begun what would turn out to be a daily ritual of doing readings for myself. With Dee as my mentor, I also learned to intuit further by reading for her and Ann on a regular basis too. The more I worked on developing my intuitive skills the more I realized I did not want anything to hinder my abilities, so I quit taking diet pills. It was the not knowing for sure what affects, if any, they might be having on my mind and body that I thought it best to give them up.

Hence, the weight returned, and I felt sluggish. Dee and Ann suggested a remedy for me that I was not too crazy about at first - hiking. According to Dee, connecting with Mother Earth was going to be another way for me to improve my intuitive powers. So with that in mind, I found myself huffing and puffing up mountain trails while silently cussing at Dee and Ann under my breath. However, the more time I spent in Mother Nature, the more I came to appreciate her natural beauty. By becoming aware of my surroundings, I realized too that the Universe was communicating with me on a daily basis through visualization and symbolism. The more receptive I was to trust in her messages, the more I was willing to let Spirit guide me. This in turn led me to practice the Taoist concept of Wu Wei, living in the "flow."

The one drawback to Wu Wei, however, is that it requires a lot of patience to let things unfold according to God's plan. In time, as my faith grew stronger to believe in this concept, I learned not to worry about how things were going to turn out because deep down inside I knew I would always be provided for.

Thus, by attaining this new inner confidence, I had become comfortable with having quit my job and taking the needed time off to go to Sedona to rejuvenate my mind, body and spirit before beginning my new business venture. Plus, I also realized that by living alone I was able to stay focused on my self-discovery program, and that I had become more self-assured in the decisions I had made up to this point — that is until the day Dee did a reading for me while we were still in Sedona.

The day before we were to head back to San Diego, I was in tears, and I wasn't quite sure if it was out of happiness or sadness. Because, according to Dee's reading, there was still a strong chance my marriage could be saved. Since Dee was my mentor, I believed what she had told me to be true. Maybe she was right. Maybe what I had been searching for all along had been the spiritual link. So without deliberation, I called Joe to tell him the good news that I had changed my mind once again about getting a divorce. Inconveniently though, Joe's parents had just arrived earlier that day from Tennessee, and he was in the midst of telling them about our upcoming divorce when I phoned. "Well tell them there's a possibility we may not be getting one." I said. "Let's go away for the weekend when I get back so we can talk about it."

"You'll have a lot of explaining to do." Joe said.

"I don't think so," was my reply. "I've found what's been missing in my life and everything is going to be okay."

Leaving Sedona the next day to head back home, we mapped out our return to San Diego via Las Vegas. We continued to write our desires out ahead of time and the Universe continued to deliver.

Journal Entry May 7, 1996

"Please provide us with a safe and secure trip back to San Diego. Please let it be harmonious, and let us find a nice quiet place in Las Vegas for the night."

Midafternoon we arrived in Las Vegas. Sightseeing, shopping and eating — this last night of our vacation was probably one of the best times we ever spent together. We laughed so much it hurt. We had become the best of friends.

The following day I was back in Joe's arms telling him all about my wonderful experiences during the trip and the power of writing things out ahead of time which he found hard to believe.

"We'll write out our desires before we leave for our weekend together." I said, hoping to provide him proof of my convictions. As an example, since Joe forgot to specify a king size bed when he had made reservations, I took care of it in my written request:

"May Joe's and my room for tonight have a beautiful view, king-size bed, and be very quiet. May it be very safe and secure."

Once again, the Universe provided us with everything we had asked for, plus we received a bonus in the morning - viewing a glorious sunrise upon our awakening.

That weekend, having convinced Joe my search to what was missing in my life was over, he took me back. However, bruising my ego, he also informed me he needed to break up with a woman he had been seeing since I moved out. Suddenly, a new insecure feeling had come over me when I realized Joe had not wasted any time in finding someone else. Recognizing I was extremely jealous of my husband's relationship with another woman, I also came to realize too that "karma" had prevailed — what goes around, comes around. After all, it was only fair that I should experience what Joe had felt about my relationship with Ray. With that realization, I decided to make one last call to Ray telling him about my reconciliation with Joe and to say goodbye.

Having recommitted to my marriage once again, I moved back in with Joe the end of May, cancelled our divorce proceedings, and said goodbye to Ray for the last time. Henceforth, I had hoped all of us could put the past behind us and get on with our lives. Unfortunately, that was not to be the case. Unforeseen turmoil was yet to come.

Already the beginning of June, two months after Dee had started working on her new presentation, Ann and I were anxiously awaiting to hold our first seminar so we could start recouping some of the monies we had spent thus far on our partnership, which also included paying all of Dee's monthly living expenses since April so she could devote the majority of her time putting the new program together. However, Dee was still not ready, and other factors too caused us further delays.

Consequently, with no money coming in from my new business venture, my "nest egg" from refinancing the house was being depleted much faster than I had anticipated. With some growing concern, Joe started to question my ability to meet future financial obligations if I continued with my new business venture; so much so, that he had begun to strongly suggest I consider finding a "real" job.

Except going back to the corporate world was not what I wanted. I believed in my new company and the message we wanted to convey to others about developing their intuitive powers. More importantly, I wanted to be able to live in the "flow" and trust in the Universe to provide.

Therefore, I had no intentions of giving up.

Yet, I also knew to listen to my inner voice, and lately it was trying to tell me that something was amiss. However, because I had allowed my thoughts to become scattered, I was unable to discern what it was. Gradually, I was losing the connection to my Higher Power by letting other influences affect my thought process. Pangs of jealousy were surfacing in my feelings for Joe causing me to wonder if he had truly severed his relationship with the "other" woman. Then, to add more confusion to my state of mind, the subject of money was now becoming an issue between us.

Yet, I believed once Dee, Ann and I held our first seminar, the money would start rolling in. So I kept reassuring Joe, and myself, that everything was going to be okay. Boy! What a misstatement that turned out to be!

Intuitively speaking, I was not. My new company was in trouble, and I had not seen it coming. From day one, I had unknowingly created a major blockage to my inner voice by allowing Dee, who was not business oriented, to call the majority of the shots regarding the company because I believed her "Higher Power" to be more developed than my own. In addition, because Ann and I believed that Dee had spiritual guides to provide us with insight, we thought we were assured of a successful business. Therefore, upon Dee's instructions, Ann and I were asked not to meet or make any decisions without her. Foolishly, and until it was too late to remedy the situation, we had listened and obeyed.

Scheduling times when the three of us were going to meet on a regular basis proved to be a little more difficult than we had anticipated. Family obligations began to surface upon our return from Sedona, and we all agreed that these would take precedence over company business, at least for the time being. However, this agreement almost led to the demise of our partnership before it even got started due to the fact that Dee and I felt Ann had taken on one obligation too many that might interfere with the business — taking care of her grandchildren.

Unbeknownst to Dee and I one of Ann's daughters was arriving from Boise the end of May to intern for a law firm during the summer months. However, the fact that she was also bringing her two young daughters with her for Ann to watch while she worked had not come to light until after we had gone into partnership together. As Dee and I did not want babysitting to become a part of our job function, we were ready to give Ann an ultimatum to either make other arrangements on the days were conducting business, or we would dissolve the partnership. However, the night before discussing this with her, a dream I had helped me to change my mind.

I was driving down a busy street on a motorcycle when I saw a toddler, approximately 18 months old. As I was going too fast to stop, I left it up to someone else behind me to save the child. As I proceeded, another toddler was out in the street. This time I stopped. I picked the child up and handed him to his mother. I regretted handing the baby back to the mother as she was not comforting the child but yelling at him. I was so angry at the mother. I felt the baby needed to be comforted instead, and that she was to blame in the first place because she did not supervise her child.

When I picked Dee up the following morning to go to Ann's, I relayed my dream to her. Ironically, Dee also dreamt about unsupervised children where she too had been angry with the parents. Strange, Dee was riding a bike in her dream.

Both of us had decided to softened our attitudes toward the situation because we knew how much

Ann loved her little girls. It was a time for compassion, and the three of us would find a way to work things out to everyone's satisfaction.

Another delay was the paperwork. Since Ann's daughter was studying to be a lawyer, we waited for her arrival so she could go over the Limited Liability Partnership form with us before filing it with the state. Even still, we ended up having to resubmit it as we had inadvertently left some information off. Finally, in July our company had become a reality.

With the creation of our partnership, another problem arose - egos. Dee and I would continuously argue as to which direction the company should go. She kept insisting upon being the "star." Anytime the spotlight was taken away from her, she resented it. She felt it was the company I was promoting and not her. It was true. Ann and I were looking at the larger picture - we eventually hoped to promote many stars, not just one. Dee could never understand that she had a lot to gain if we sponsored other speakers. After all, she was the company too.

Then again, why even argue if we had nothing to promote yet. Dee was taking longer than Ann and I had anticipated in preparing her material. In addition, before going public, we wanted Dee to do a test run for us. She complied, and after hearing her presentation, we were satisfied. Ann and I thought Dee had the potential to be a very good speaker. However, we felt she still needed more grooming. We decided to tape her first workshop and go over it with her later.

Almost three months after quitting my job, we held our first seminar. One person attended.

Against my better judgment, we went ahead and scheduled two more seminars for the following week. I wanted to wait until our company stationery was ready so we could send out flyers. Instead, Dee wanted us to call people. She supplied us with a list of her tarot clientele to contact, and we would also ask family and friends to come. Personally, I disliked phone soliciting intensely. Nonetheless, to my chagrin, I called.

For the time being, we had reserved Dee's apartment complex clubhouse to hold the seminars. With a refundable deposit, there was no charge for the room. Our very first non-paying guest was Ann's daughter-in-law. The company's policy was to let any family members attend for free. Dee gave her presentation and then the four of us went to lunch.

The feedback to Dee was not good. Ann said there were parts of the program her daughter-in-law felt did not flow smoothly. Ann had recorded and transcribed the tape to go over with her. Dee was not a happy camper. She felt any input from us was too critical. Her ego had been deflated.

Before the seminar I had written my "request" to the Universe for a good turnout. I felt the Universe would only provide if we were ready. To me, it was a sign that we weren't. The following week was the same thing. Again, the Universe was telling us we were still not ready. One guest showed up. A friend of Dee's. No seminar. He took us out to lunch instead. Still not wanting to wait to mail out flyers, Dee asked us to run an ad in a local newspaper using her name only - no mention of the company's. Again, we complied with her request. Another seminar was held on a Sunday. Again one person showed up - a friend of Ann's. We all left early.

At this point, Ann and I realized we needed to start making the business decisions; and, if need be, just the two of us would meet to discuss strategies. We also agreed it was important to wait for the company stationery and business cards in order to present ourselves and the company in a professional manner. The printers called August 9th. Finally, the company was ready to go, but Dee wasn't.

Besides lacking confidence, Dee also had doubts about Ann and I. She had every reason too. Lately, whenever Dee and I did tarot readings for each other, the cards were revealing only two partners instead of three, but which two? Dee believed there was no company without her. So that left either Ann or myself. Would it be me because I had the confidence she lacked? Or would it be Ann because she was easier going than I was? At this point it really didn't matter anymore; Dee doubted both of us. One minute she thought Ann was working against her; the next minute she thought I was. If we couldn't trust each other, then for sure our partnership was doomed, but not the company.

With Ann leaving for Europe in a couple of weeks, we decided it was a good time to take a break from each other. We would regroup when she got back to plan our next step. However, during Ann's absence Dee told me she didn't think the company was going to succeed. That's when I realized I could not depend upon her or anyone else for my success — it had to come from within. I did not feel defeated, but she did.

When Ann returned, the three of us met at Dee's to conduct what would be our last business meeting. It was Dee who requested out of the partnership. No problem. Ann and I would keep the company. We weren't sure what we were going to do with it yet, but first we needed to get Dee's name removed as an officer of the company. Ann and I decided to meet the following week for lunch to discuss which direction we wanted to go; maybe we would make this a part-time venture instead.

A few days before our luncheon, I had agreed to do a tarot reading for Jean, the owner of the hair salon where I frequented. For the past couple of months she had been after me to do a reading for her. However, confessing to being a novice, I kept recommending Dee to her instead. Jean was persistent. She wanted me to do her reading and no one else. Finally, I complied by agreeing to an exchange - a haircut for a reading.

Jean's feedback had been very encouraging. According to her, my interpretation of the cards had been very accurate and helpful. Afterwards I thought to myself "maybe I could do this for a living." Sometime ago, Dee had predicted my doing readings for others too. "I don't think so," had been my reply. Now I was thinking maybe I would. Ann also helped. Since she was going to look for another job, she suggested my using the company to promote myself. It was an idea I was considering, but just when I was getting ready to "go for it," my inner voice had a different message for me. I just didn't know if I had the strength or courage to listen to it.

An urgency came over me to move back to Chicago. I felt like I was on a timeframe and it was imperative I return at once. Confiding in Ann, she and I decided to go ahead and dissolve the company.

Once again, I broke the news to Joe that something was still missing. This time no explanations were required. We filed for divorce. The direction of my life had taken another turn. I was headed towards Chicago; I was going home to be with my family.

The Higher Power Within

—◄o►—

T HE NINE INSIGHTS REVEALED in **"The Celestine Prophecy"** inspired me to start reaching out to others with love in my heart, and to put all my faith and trust in God. Beginning with the first insight of recognizing the importance of "meaningful coincidences," to the last insight of evolving into a spiritual being, I realized my life had taken on new meaning, and I liked the person I was becoming.

Even though there had been a lot of heartache up to this point, I believed it was all essential in order for me to learn some valuable lessons about love and life. Discovering what those lessons were, I had to go back in time and understand my past. Thus, by coming face-to-face with Ray again, I had learned to heal old wounds, and in doing so it no longer hurt anymore to know I still loved him. In fact, I wouldn't have traded that experience for anything in the world; it just helped to reinforce the saying "It's better to have loved and lost than never to have loved at all." I was ready to love again, and the person I needed to begin with was me.

I decided to work on those areas that I did not like about myself - starting with my intimidating personality. Having grown up with two brothers and two sisters, I use to threaten them with bodily harm to get my way. Once in a while I would have to prove myself, but then over time just saying it was enough. Words had become power for me at a very young age.

Also, I strove to be a perfectionist, which led me to expect a lot from myself and from others. By placing more emphasis on results than I was on a person's feelings, however, I sometimes found myself becoming alienated from the very people I was trying to help.

My obsession in having to control everything in my life had carried over into my trying to control others too. With so many things to deal with and so many people to worry about, I had become stressed to the point where I no longer wanted to control anymore.

The day I decided to relinquish control was the day Dee requested out of the company. At first, my reaction had been that of a raving lunatic when I heard she wanted to quit. Screaming at the top of my lungs, I blamed her for everything – her lack of trust in Ann and I to make any decisions without her; her taking too long to put together the new program; and her lack of confidence in herself. Still yelling, I told her I was sick and tired of trying to build up her confidence when she had none. Dee, on the other hand, and a lot more composed than I was, felt Ann and I had failed to promote her and that the company was doomed.

Believing no amount of arguing would have convinced Dee otherwise, I decided to surrender.

Without warning, I had stopped ranting and raving. Calm and no longer angry, Dee and Ann stared in disbelief at my sudden transformation; I'm sure they were both wondering if I had completely lost it. On the contrary, it was at the moment of surrender, when I had let go of ego, I had felt His presence throughout my entire body, from my head to my toes, cleansing my heart and soul. He was taking over my life without any struggle from me, and now, with God in control, I was at peace.

Angel Readings, Numerology And Tarot

—◄○►—

IT WAS ON A Friday the 13th when I had asked Joe a third time for a divorce. The following Monday we signed the papers, and two days later I was on the road headed towards Chicago with $800.00 in cash, some clothes, tarot cards, books, and my angel collection. Surprisingly, even though I didn't have a clue as to what I was going to do once I got there, I was not afraid.

Temporarily, I had planned to stay with my mother until I could find a place to live. I didn't have to wait long. The lady who lived directly above my mother was moving to Arizona and her apartment was going to be available in a few weeks. I met with the owners of the building who also resided on site and they told me the apartment was mine if I wanted it. In addition, the owners, along with my mother, offered to help me furnish it until I was ready to go back to San Diego to get my things which Joe had graciously offered to keep for me until I was settled.

Living in the "flow" was truly working out for me. I didn't have to fill out any lease papers, the rent was very reasonable, and my mother lived directly below me so I could borrow whatever I needed. Plus, the Universe had provided another bonus – the apartment came with a garage, a big plus for the upcoming winter months.

As easy as it was to find a place to live, I wasn't as confident about finding a job. Thus, being unsure of which direction to go, I decided to sign up with a temporary employment agency. However, after arriving home after filling out the paperwork and taking several tests, I began to cry because I truly did not want to go back to the corporate world. "Dear God, please help me." I prayed.

Soon after my request, I heard from my mother that there was a metaphysical store close by where they had tarot readers. Days later, I was interviewing with Fred and Gail, owners of the store for a position as a tarot reader. To test my abilities, I was required to do readings for each of them to see if they felt I was qualified. I too wanted to know, "Was I?"

Up until now, the only people I had done readings for were Dee, Ann, and Jean, my hairdresser whose feedback had been very positive. I also remember Jean telling me she especially liked it when I concluded her reading with an angel message.

Believing that nothing happens by accident, the day before Jean's reading I had gone to buy more tarot cards. This time, however, I was going to pick my next deck of cards intuitively, and I had a lot to choose from. From behind the counter, I had the store clerk show me almost every deck of tarot cards. Then, towards the very back, I saw them. They were the only angel oracle cards there. From that day on, I included them in my readings.

Ready to be tested, and with cards in hand, I did readings for Fred and Gail. I felt if God wanted me at their store then all would go well. It did. They agreed to give me a try and, based upon what I made, they would collect a commission fee. My first day on the job was two weeks later. I had one reading and made $10.50, after paying the fee. I was thrilled to death! My new career had begun. I went from secretary, office manager, co-owner of a business, to becoming a tarot reader. Unbelievable!

Fortunately, for the time being anyway, I was not going to have to depend on my earnings from doing readings. Before starting my job as an intuitive consultant, I drove back to San Diego to spend a week with Joe and to pick up more clothes and dishes. Joe also had graciously agreed to give me part of my settlement right away.

Without having to worry about money, I was able to explore other interests too, namely, numerology and writing. Somehow I always knew numerology was going to be a part of my life. Ever since I can remember, I had the habit of adding people's birthdates in my head, and I also knew the esoteric meaning of some of the numbers. I didn't know how I knew these things; I just did.

I bought my first numerology book when Dee, Ann and I stopped at a book store in Sedona. With numerous books on the subject, I intuitively selected my book by asking the sales clerk if she had a list of all the numerology books in the store. She did and when she showed the list to me I was drawn to one book in particular. Without even opening it when she handed it to me, I bought **"Numerology and The Divine Triangle,"** by Faith Javane and Dusty Bunker. Six months later, I opened it and began studying this ancient science and the hidden meaning of numbers. From this book, I also discovered the correlation between numbers, Tarot and Astrology which led me to exploring the predictability of life experiences by associating numbers with tarot cards and astrological energies.

In addition, I also learned that by adding the month, day and year of my birthday together determines my **Life Lesson Number** which provides insight as to my cosmic gifts, life lessons and the progression of my spiritual journey (i.e. June 10, 1952: 6 + 10 + 1+9+5+2 = 33). In Tarot, the number 33 is represented by the

Seven of Wands. However, there are many ways to interpret a tarot card. Here are just a few inner meanings of the number 33 and its respective tarot card : The Master Teacher (I always wanted to be a teacher), Courage to stand up for one's beliefs, Self-Sacrifice, Commitments, Compassion, Family Responsibilities, Religious and moral standards. Later on, I would discover the importance of my **Life Lesson Number 33**.

Wanting to share what I had learned from these ancient tools, I signed up to teach Community Education classes. Little by little, more and more people were finding out what I did for a living. However, some friends and relatives frowned upon my new chosen career. Admitting to using these ancient tools was like "coming out of the closet." Although there are those who believe tarot and numerology are the work of the devil, I believe they have provided me with a greater understanding of my past, present and hopefully my future.

In addition to learning my Life Lesson Number from my birthday, I also learned my birth name uncovers three other personal spiritual numbers as well.

By adding the vowels in my given name at birth and using the following numeric code for the alphabet (A=1, E=5, I=9, O=6,

U=3), my **Soul Number 18** is determined and reveals past karma and what I hope to resolve in this lifetime.

$$\underline{1 \quad 1} \qquad \underline{9 \; 1} \quad \underline{6} = 18$$

S A R A H B. D I A M O N D

In Tarot, the number 18 is represented by **The Moon.** Here are just a few interpretations for this tarot card: Dreams, worrying about the unknown, authenticity, relationship with Pisces individuals (those born February 18 – March 20).

Having discovered 18 as my Soul Number, I was able to gain some insight as to why I was having a reoccurring nightmare as a child. This dream came and went over a period of time. Nothing but faces appearing one at a time. First they started off in the distance surrounded by fog, and then they would get closer and closer - very old, ghost-like faces. They never said anything, they just frightened me.

I couldn't believe how accurate the description was for the number 18 in "**Numerology and The Divine Triangle:**" "As a child you may have had nightmares…fears in the form of monsters chasing you in your dreams."

With no more monsters haunting me, I discovered the man of my dreams. By adding the consonants in my given name at birth using the following numeric code for the alphabet reveals my **Outside Influences Number 37** - The King of Hearts.

Consonant numeric code: B=2, C=3, D=4, F=6, G=7, H=8, J=1, K=2, L=3, M=4, N=5, P=7, Q=8, R=9, S=1, T=2, V=4, W=5, X=6, Y=7, Z=8.

$$\underline{1 \quad 9 \quad 8 \quad 2 \quad 4 \quad\quad 4 \quad 5 \quad 4} = 37$$

S A R A H B. D I A M O N D

In Tarot the number 37 represents the King of Hearts, an astrological water sign male: Cancer, those born 6/21-7/22, Scorpio (10/23 – 11/21) or Pisces (2/20 – 3/20). Maybe that's why my first two serious relationships were with water sign males. I lost my virginity to a Scorpio at age 18, and I left him for another Scorpio whom I ended up living with for a short time. Then a few years later there was my relationship with Ray, the Pisces.

Finally, by adding my Soul Number 18 to my Outside Influences Number 37, I discovered my **Destiny Number 55**. This number is associated with The Ace of Swords tarot card and, according to the description in **"Numerology and The Divine Triangle,"** I could be a writer and "a pioneer in the realm of thoughts..."

Oh, the power of my thoughts...

The Thought Process

TIME ALONE. TIME TO think. Time for reflection.

"If I only knew then what I know now." This adage came to mind as I thought about Ray.

It had been over four months since Ray and I had last spoken to each other. Ray had been trying to reach me but when he had discovered the phone numbers he had to my previous job and apartment were no longer valid, he decided to contact my sister, Faith to find me. She relayed his message to me and one week later, after Joe and I had filed for a divorce, I was back in Chicago.

I returned his call the following day I arrived in town. "Hi." "Got your message you were looking for me. Any chance you're coming to Chicago soon?" I asked.

"As a matter of fact, I am." He said. "Tomorrow."

I had truly loved him. So why then didn't things worked out between us? Was this another one of God's lessons for me to learn

— giving my heart so completely only to experience having it broken?

I don't think God works that way, but energy vibrations do. Absolutely everything in the Universe is comprised of energy. Everything evolves from energy. As a student of metaphysics, I realize how important thoughts are. Thoughts affect energy vibrations and the ability to tap into a higher consciousness, mainly one's intuitive link. Positive thoughts produce higher vibrations and negative thoughts produce lower vibrations which can cause blockages to one's sixth sense.

At the beginning of my relationship with Ray, my sixth sense, intuition, was very active. Invariably, I knew when he was thinking about me and when he was going to call. It's the closest thing to mental telepathy I had ever experienced. I also realized, the more in sync we were with each other's thoughts, the stronger my intuition became. Sometimes I would experiment and send him "thought" messages that I wanted him to call. Many times it worked. He also had the ability to reach me in my thoughts, and I would answer. I also recognized that by having the ability to allow him into my thoughts, I also had the ability to keep him out. Now he was back.

"So, what happened?" "Why are you back in Chicago?" Ray asked nervously.

"Don't worry," I said. "I am not doing this because of you. I did it knowing you would not be there for me. Your children are the most important thing in your life, and I would never do anything to hurt you or your family. I am following my heart, and, for whatever reason, it has led me back here."

"So where do we go from here?" He asked.

I responded as honestly as I could. "I don't know. Let's just take it one day at a time."

1997

I T'S HARD FOR ME to believe it's been almost two years since this saga began. Several times I almost faltered and went back to where I felt safe. Occasionally, I ventured back to Joe's comforting arms to where I was reassured he still cared about me.

With 1996 soon coming to an end, the last three months had proved to be very difficult for me. Even though my family was close by, I felt isolated and withdrawn. Ray and I had spoken only once since I moved back. While staying at my mother's for two weeks, he had tried calling me several times, but I always missed him. Then after I moved into my apartment and had my phone installed, I called and left my new number with his secretary. Again while I was out, he called and left a message on my voice mail. I would replay his message over and over again just to hear his voice. After a while though listening to a recording was wearing thin; I wanted to talk to him. It had been over a week since he left the message. Depression was setting in and I realized I was holding on to tight and needed to let go. I erased his message. Two minutes later the phone rang. It was him.

That was the last time I spoke to Ray in 1996. Being this close to each other was uncomfortable for both of us. He didn't call anymore and neither did I. Instead I chose to concentrate on my career.

As a tarot reader, I discovered another important lesson. Being judgmental can hinder intuitive guidance if it is based on a person's looks or profession. Therefore, I preferred to wait until after their readings to learn more about them. Sometimes I was totally flabbergasted — stripper, professor, cross-dresser, doctor, minister, etc. It was a great way to meet a lot of interesting people.

I also discovered some people were amazed at my ability to intuitively tap into their thought waves and express what they were thinking. Now, listening to my own thought waves, I felt the need to connect with Ray again. However, I did not want to talk to him. It was the end of 1996 and I only wanted to wish him a Happy New Year so I called very early in the morning to leave a message on his voice mail. Surprise! He answered, and I hung up. How juvenile I thought to myself. Besides, remembering nothing is by accident, I redialed.

"Did you just call and hang up?" He asked.

"That was me. I really didn't want to talk to you. I was just going to leave a message saying I had been thinking about you during the holidays and also to wish you well for the New Year."

He confessed he had been thinking about me too and didn't know how to handle our relationship. We both wondered if it would be possible to meet once in a while for a cup of coffee. Ray and I agreed to see each other the next time he was in town. He thought around the 20th of January.

We also discussed careers. He had asked me what I was doing and I confessed that I was delving into the unknown again. Years ago he hadn't believed in such things. What about now? He too had changed. He was open minded to learning more about my new life, but he politely declined when I offered to do a reading for him. "Maybe another time" he said. Even though he was still skeptical about being able to see into the future, I assured him I would not look into his without permission.

I was looking forward to the New Year. In addition to getting to see Ray again, I was going to teach my first numerology class in January 1997. Through the promotions of my mother and sister, I had eight students. As my apartment would become my classroom, preparations needed to be made to get a computer so I could devise worksheets and set up an accounting system for my business. The

Universe had responded to my first request for a computer, maybe it would do so again for a second one.

Some time ago, after receiving my message at the vortex to "write," I had asked the Universe to furnish me with a computer. "Dear God, please provide me with a free computer and printer so that I may begin my novel." Even though it took several months, the Universe responded to my request. I received **exactly** what I had asked for.

When I moved back to Chicago, Faith gave me a computer and printer she wasn't using. Unfortunately, it was very outdated and did not have a hard drive. Writing to the Universe was tricky business; I had to be careful how I requested things. With no time to waste, I decided to go ahead and buy a used one. I put it out to the Universe that I was looking for a computer and printer at a reasonable price and to be everything I needed. Faith called to let me know there was an ad in the paper for an IBM 486 PS/1, 3 years old, color monitor and printer - $600. Sold!

Everything was ready except, instead of celebrating, I found myself crying. Wednesday, the day before class, my divorce papers had arrived in the mail. I called Ray. He was going to be leaving town the following Wednesday. "Maybe we could get together Monday or Tuesday?" He asked.

"Sure. Just give me a call." I said.

It wasn't meant to be. Joe had just gotten our divorce papers. "It's ironic," he said. "The divorce date is the same as my first divorce." My heart went out to him, but now was not a good time to talk as my students were getting ready to leave. He said he would call me back the next day. The phone rang early in the morning. Joe was having a difficult time dealing with the divorce. I asked him if he needed me and he said "Yes." I told him I would check on flights right away.

I booked a flight out Monday morning and I called Ray to let him know I was flying back to San Diego for a week. We then planned to get together when we both got back from our trips. However, time was not on our side; the day we planned to meet, his son needed him to attend a school function.

Even though I wanted to see Ray more than anything else, I knew as long as there were blockages stopping us from seeing each other, our getting together was not meant to be. I found solace in my daily angel and tarot readings. According to my inner feelings, I believed everything was going to be okay. For now I would concentrate on my work and helping others. At the store, I was meeting a lot of interesting people. Whenever available, I offered free angel advice to anyone who wanted it. Hope stopped by. She was the business manager for a local health club where they specialized in massage therapy training and yoga. We talked about readings and numerology.

"Do you teach numerology classes?" she asked. "Would you be interested in teaching at our facility?"

I couldn't believe it. The Universe was providing for me once again. What an opportunity. There was so much potential because they had a large clientele list. Hope and I set up an appointment to go over the details. They would handle everything - sending out flyers, taking reservations, collecting the money, and paying my fee. She just needed to confirm everything with the owner of the institute. Tentatively, we scheduled two classes, one in March and another one in April. The following week after our meeting, Hope called to apologize. The owner did not want to go that route. I told her not to worry about it; something else would come along as I believed the Universe would always provide for me. I did wonder, however, if this had been a message for me to do something else. Should I be thinking about teaching numerology on a larger scale? I decided to talk to Ann to see what she thought. Maybe we could go into partnership again. Monday, February 17th, I called her.

Ann did not want to get into another business venture. She had other plans; she was getting married the following month.

However, she did offer me some advice. "I don't think you should be thinking about another business right now. You should be concentrating on your creative talents; teach and write - go with the flow! You have the ability to touch others," Ann said. "I think you should write your book now." I decided to take Ann's advice. I started writing my book the following day.

The Pursuit For Fulfillment

◄O►

S ECOND CHANCES. MY LIFE began again when I started listening
to my "inner voice" and to my heart. By being completely
honest with myself and others, it changed the course of my life.
However, it wasn't easy making some of the decisions I made. I had
to face certain fears such as monetary security, being alone again,
and possibly losing the love of the two men I cared most about.
With God's help, I was able to conquer my fears.

I no longer worried about losing Joe's love. Even after everything
we had been through, we still loved each other. We kept the lines
of communication opened between us and on occasion I would go
to San Diego to see him. Fortunately for me, having to let Joe go in
order for me to grow could be done gradually.

Having to let Ray go too was another matter. My intuition and
heart were telling me not to and I chose to listen to them.

It had been a month and a half since Ray and I talked. On St.
Patrick's Day around 5:30 p.m., I had a strong desire to phone him

at the office. I believed if I was meant to talk to him, he would be there; if not, he would be gone. He was there and we talked for 1/2 hour. His father's health was ailing, and he had taken several trips out-of-state to be with him. He also talked a little about his children and tried to keep the conversation light and said we would talk again soon.

He called me the day his father died.

Days prior to that, I had taken my mother and grandmother to the airport to catch the first flight out to Boston. Later that morning my mother called. "Guess who I just talked to?" She said. "Ray. He's on his way to see his father who's not doing too well. Too bad you didn't get to see him when you dropped us off." I couldn't believe it. I had been that close to him. Still, something was keeping us apart.

Later that evening he called. His father had passed away that morning. It had been a long time since he and I had a serious conversation. He touched my heart and soul and I missed him terribly.

Two weeks later, I had this gut feeling something was wrong with Ray so I called him. His secretary had been instructed not to put anyone through, but she recognized my voice and asked me to hold. He took my call.

"Hi, are you okay?" I asked.

"Why, did my numbers come up bad?" he inquired.

I laughed. "No. I was just worried about you."

"Can I call you back?" he asked.

"No problem," I said.

Later that day he called and told me he wanted a divorce.

Divine Guidance

I BELIEVE WE ARE GIVEN many chances to discover the path of our destiny if we are willing to develop and listen to the devices God has given us. The **MIND** holds the key to our direct link to Him — intuition, whereas the **BODY** houses the heart where all our emotions lie and tells us if we are whole, and then we have each other to help guide us along our **SPIRIT**ual journey.

Thus, by learning to develop and trust my intuition, along with meditating and listening to my heart, the real me began to emerge. By listening to my "inner guidance," I also discovered the path back to my destiny — the path back to God. Soon, my mission in life had become clear in that I wanted to help others discover their true selves as well.

To help others, though, I realized I had to be whole, and signals from the heart had told me I was not. The emotional turmoil I had experienced from seeing Ray again had been the indicator that something was out of sync in my life. From there, however, after healing the past, I was then able to get back on track. Plus, going back in time had also proved very beneficial in helping me to understand the progression of my spiritual journey.

Yet, some questions still remained unanswered. Why would the angels tell me to go to Ray when he was married and so was I. Obviously, I loved Joe too. Otherwise, why would I have asked the angels to watch over Joe when I had my "past life experience."

Could it be that Ray, Joe and I were involved in each other's mission here on earth? According to Angel, the three of us were soul mates. To add confirmation to what Angel had told me, I remembered a passage in the book **"Embraced By The Light,"** by Betty J. Eadie that said pretty much the same thing.

Whatever Joe, Ray and I had to learn, whatever karma we brought into this life, it gave me comfort to believe the three of us agreed to our experiences prior to coming here. I would accept whatever payback I deserved with a greater understanding to move forward in love and light.

Thinking of karma, I thought back to when I was in first grade and several of my friends and I were being very mischievous and the teacher had caught us. One by one, we were reprimanded, and when it was my turn, the nun said: "Sarah, the other girls look up to you as their leader. Try setting a better example for them to follow." Wow, what pressure. I didn't know if I wanted to be the leader or not.

I chose to lead. In high school I found myself back in front of other classmates again, this time teaching instead as I was asked to participate in student/teacher day. Years later, standing in front of my first numerology class, I reflected back to this memory.

My life, however, wouldn't have changed much if I hadn't started reaching out to others for help. Angel's counsel had taught me the importance of journaling; from Dee I had learned to develop my Higher Power; Ann's love and support had guided me in the direction to teach and write; and Fred and Gail, owners of the metaphysical store where I did tarot readings were instrumental in launching my new career. These were just a few people who played key roles in my life; and now, through my counseling, I discovered I was playing a key role in other lives too — even Ray's.

Ray and I rarely ever talked about our marriages because what we shared with our spouses we considered to be a private matter. However, now Ray was confiding in me that he wanted a divorce. For months, he had been struggling with his unhappiness, and he had even wondered if he was going through a mid-life crisis. Having done his numerology chart, I knew he was under a heavy-duty vibration during the month of April and only by looking within was he going to find what he was looking for.

Even though Ray wanted a divorce did not mean it was imminent as he was struggling with how he was going to tell his children. Ray decided to seek professional counseling which I thought was a good idea too, because where Ray was concerned, I couldn't be objective.

Just as Ray was going to seek guidance, I too chose to ask for help from God. The following day I went to the lake to meditate.

Sitting at my usual spot off the path, a young boy and his dog walked down to where I was. He had been riding his bike and was now maneuvering it down the rocks. He laid his bike down in front of me and removed his helmet. Casually, as he started toward the lake, he asked me not to steal it. I laughed and told him not to worry. I watched as his dog swam in the water and within a few minutes they were back and the dog was shaking water all over me.

"Isn't it too cold for him to be in the water?" I asked.

He looked at me and said, "You're not from around here are you."

"I just moved back." I answered.

"Where are you from?" he wanted to know.

"San Diego," I offered.

"I have a friend who lives in San Diego. Why did you move back here." he asked.

Inquisitive little thing, I told him it was to be close to my family and because I liked being near the water.

"Yeah. It's neat here." he replied while putting his helmet back on.

"It's nice that you enjoy it so much; riding your bike and taking your dog swimming."

Heading back up the hill, I heard him say, "Well, I'm not going to be a kid forever. I have to enjoy it while I can."

I smiled and whispered to myself, "Yes, I guess you're not going to be a child forever."

Walking back to my car, the "voice within" said, "talk to the children."

Then I remembered **<u>The Celestine Prophecy,</u>** mentioned children. It was part of the Eighth Insight - the importance of communicating with children and being truthful with them. The next day I called Ray to share this "insight" with him.

"Just be honest and tell them the truth." I said.

Ray's anguish was apparent. He understood the need to talk to them; he just didn't know how to start.

"Have you read "**<u>The Celestine Prophecy</u>**"? I asked. This book helped change my life. Maybe it can help you too. I will send you my copy today."

Three weeks later I called Ray to see what he thought of the book, but to my surprise he had not read it yet. Then more time had passed without any action on his part. It was here I had originally intended to end my story, with the hopes that someday Ray would find inspiration from the same book I had.

I called to let him know I had finished my manuscript and that I was now ready to move forward and let go of the past and of him. It was then that he had asked if he could read what I had written.

The following day, after nine months of being apart, Ray was in my apartment.

True Love

O N A TUESDAY IN June, with just a couple of hours to spare before he had to attend a meeting in town, Ray sat in my living room to read the first draft of my manuscript while I tried reading a book in another room. Painstakingly, I awaited his reaction to what I had written. From the look on his face when he had finished, I could tell Ray was visibly upset by what he had read.

"So what did you think?" I asked nervously.

Ray did not want to answer me. Instead, he asked if he could call me later after having some time to digest everything.

"Just tell me this." I pleaded. "Were my statements accurate? Is there anything written in the book about you that I need to change?"

"No." He said. "There is nothing you need to change. I'll call you later." Then he left.

Days passed without a word. Anxiety began to take over awaiting his input regarding my manuscript, and when I couldn't wait any longer, I called him. It was not good. From Ray's input, I had learned that I had failed miserably in my first attempts at writing. What I had hoped to convey to him and to others was the importance of becoming whole through self-discovery. However, Ray's perception had been clouded because to him it was not a story at all — it was about us and the reality was that he believed my marriage had ended because of my feelings for him.

I admitted to Ray that my love for him, at first, had been the catalyst for my leaving Joe, but in the end it had not been the deciding factor that had led me to venture off on my own. Over and over again, just as I had done with Joe too, I tried to explain to Ray that there had been something else missing in my life, and it wasn't until I had chosen to face my fears and the past that I was able to discover what it was — it was me — the person I wanted to become, someone who hoped to make a difference in the lives of others by providing insight from what I had learned about the Higher Power within. Without knowing what else to say, the conversation then came to an end.

Still feeling we left things unresolved and believing Ray had not accepted my explanation as to why I had ended my marriage, I called him back the following day to try once more to alleviate the guilt he was feeling about my divorce and to reassure him that

I wasn't looking for any type of commitment from him either. Unconvinced, however, Ray said he wanted to be able to talk to me occasionally but for me not to expect a romantic relationship between us, a comment which had sparked words of emotion from me to where I had told him I never wanted to see or talk to him again.

That phone call had taken place the end of June 1997. I called him back two weeks later to apologize for my anger and to accept his offer of friendship. He in turn said he felt better too knowing that we could keep the lines of communication opened between us. For there is a lot to be said about being friends. Having been able to remain close to Joe after our divorce had helped us both get through some very difficult moments. Nevertheless the time had come for closure as Joe was involved in a serious relationship, and he had kindly asked me to move my belongings from San Diego to Chicago.

Even though I was financially strapped, I had agreed to do so.

As Joe was planning a trip to Vegas with his girlfriend for a week in August, he suggested I come then to pick up my things. So with a few weeks to make preparations, I started writing in my journal asking God for guidance in accomplishing this task on a very limited budget.

Arranging with my mom and Faith to drive back to California with me, I then enlisted the help of my brothers, Lee and Tom, who both lived in San Diego, to help me too. Next, I called U-Haul to price trailers only to discover the weight of my car did not meet their requirements to pull one. Lee came to my rescue by offering to haul the trailer back for me using his truck instead.

However, no sooner had we decided to go this route, complications began to surface. Lee started having mechanical problems with the truck; there were time constraints as to when he and Tom would be available to pick up the trailer and load my belongings; and last but not least, there would be the additional costs for travel expenses which I had insisted upon paying for.

Uncomfortable that this arrangement was not flowing smoothly, I took it as a sign that another course of action was called for. Being on a timeframe, I still chose to wait for enlightenment before proceeding any further with my plans.

On Friday morning, August 15, 1997, I awoke with an idea as to how I might solve my current moving problem. I called an old friend, Jake, who was associated with a local car dealership. I asked him if I could trade my car in for one of lesser value and get some cash back for my upcoming move. Unsure of what deal, if any, could be made, Jake told me to meet him at the dealership to where he would introduced me to the owner. Prior to my arrival, however, Jake had already taken the liberty of telling the owner of my needs, and it appeared to me the deal had been done before I had even gotten there. Looking over my car as I drove up, the owner met me, told me how much trade-in allowance he was giving me for my car, and depending upon my choice of vehicles, the cash difference would be mine to keep. It was the fastest car transaction I have ever made in my life. Within the hour, I had traded in my 1994 Cavalier for a 1990 Lumina, which I had chosen because it appeared to be in mint condition, and more importantly, it also met U-haul's vehicle weight requirements for hauling the trailer size I needed. Plus, the owner had been very generous with a cash settlement, and he also had a trailer hitch put on my car free of charge.

As I was preparing emotionally for closure in San Diego, I was also dealing with my feelings for Ray. We were now back to communicating on a regular basis, but instead of feeling good about it, I was more depressed than ever. Ray, too, had confessed he had been suffering from depression. He said he had quit going to the marriage counselor because he felt it hadn't helped. Subsequently, though, with no changes to his present state of mind, he also told me his wife was now urging him to take anti-depressant drugs. Ray said he knew that was not the answer, he just wasn't quite sure what was.

For me, however, I knew what I wanted. It had been almost a year since I had moved back to Chicago, and during that time I had put my romantic life on hold to concentrate on my new career and to write my book. The time had come to be free to love and be loved, and with Ray that type of relationship was not possible with things the way they were. So when he called me the week before I was to leave on my trip (August 19th), I told him I was ready to let go, move on and find love once again.

Closure continued a week later as I sat alone in what use to be my home in San Diego. After arranging earlier with mom and Faith to having this one day to myself, I cried for hours thinking about my life with Joe. He had been a good husband, yet I had left him to search for something more. Believing my search had not been in vain, I did regret having to say goodbye to Joe. Seeing him again upon our arrival in town had been very emotional for me. With just a few minutes together before he had left for his girlfriend's, we had hugged and wished each other well. Stoically, I had kissed him goodbye, maintaining my composure until he drove away, then I broke down and cried.

Still, with endings there were soon to be new beginnings. I returned back to Chicago on Friday, August 29th to where I had Faith's son, Brad and a friend of his meet us at my apartment to unload the moving van. Two hours later, everything was put away and my place felt like home.

The next day, Doris, an old high school friend, had called asking if I would be interested in working that night doing readings and numerology for about 10 members of her family. Eagerly, I accepted. It was a wonderful evening until we heard Lady Diana had died in a car crash. The evening had ended with a feeling of loss.

The next day was another day of endings. Ray called. Little did I know, Ray had not been completely honest with me regarding his marriage. Things had been a lot worse than he had let on. He had been living in a motel for about a month while looking for a home to rent. Believing his marriage was finally over, Ray and I began to see each other over the next two weekends, up until the time karma had prevailed once again. Exactly one year to the day, September 18th, the day I had left Joe and headed for Chicago, Ray had chosen to leave me too. He had asked for my forgiveness in that he felt he had not tried hard enough to make his marriage work and that he was going to try once more. Having been through the same scenario myself, I told him I understood and that I loved him still.

However, I had also asked him never to contact me again unless he was divorced.

A month and a half later, he called. Yes, he was proceeding with the divorce.

Unfortunately, over the next several months as Ray's marriage drew closer to coming to an end, the more he withdrew from me too. I would see him only once in November, not at all in December, and one last time in January, 1998 when, after attending a meeting in town, he had stopped by to see how my interview with a local TV station had gone that morning. Having greeted him with a kiss, I had become sadden because there was no feeling of emotion, no passion. The depletion of energy in dealing with his divorce had left him cold.

Without energy, I had lost my connection to him. Plus, my intuitive powers were becoming further blocked because a fear had begun to surface - the fear that I had lost him for good. Deep down inside, I knew it was best to leave him alone during this transition period. Yet, my need to talk to him over rid this truth, and I decided not to "go with the flow." I called him several times over the course of the next three months to see how his divorce was progressing, only to discover more delays. Then in March, Ray had not returned one of my calls. The longer I had to wait, the more anxious I became to find out what was wrong. I finally ended up calling him again.

Ray, however, had taken me off guard when he said he did not want to talk to me because he felt the conversations always ended up going in one direction only. It seemed my love for him had become a barrier between us because he felt I wanted "all or nothing" in a relationship, and that I would not settle for anything less. He wanted "something," just not the "all." Using almost the same words he said to me on the phone back in July, Ray again told me he wanted to remain friends. This time I took what he said to mean rejection more than anything else. With tears in my eyes and a shakiness in my voice, I lashed out with words of my own, "I believed you loved me as much as I loved you. From this moment on, I will never tell you I love you again," and then I slammed the phone down.

It was a statement that made me sick. I wanted to call Ray back immediately and tell him I was sorry. Instead I chose to let him be. I was no longer sure anymore if maybe I hadn't become blinded by my love for Ray once again to becoming incapable of seeing the situation clearly. I decided then to seek the council of those who knew me best - my mother and sister. They reminded me to refocus on "living in the flow" and not forcing things to happen as I had been trying to do in my relationship with Ray.

Once again I thought about my angel message to let Ray go. Finally it had become clear. Letting Ray go was to be done out of love for if he really was my true love, I needed to trust that love would prevail.

This, however, would prove to be a test I was not sure I was going to pass.

A Test Of Faith

D AYS HAD TURNED INTO weeks; weeks had turned into months, and I still had not heard from Ray. Yet I knew he had to be thinking about me once in a while since, by "coincidence," my sister, Faith, had been placed in his path.

Ironically, the day of my last phone conversation with Ray in April, 1998 was the same day Faith had received a call from her employer asking her to attend some meetings out of town. Ray, too, was scheduled to be at those meetings.

The day of their first meeting together was the same day I was giving a talk to students at a local college about numerology. I was also hoping to drum up more business at the school as I was not making enough money to meet my monthly financial obligations. I had maxed out most of my credit cards to pursue my dream job as an intuitive consultant. Money was becoming an issue for me, and I ended up activating the last of my personal line of credit for

$6,000. Yet, I continued to have faith that things would get better, personally and financially.

Over the next several months, my sister, Faith would hear things about Ray and share them with me. According to the rumor mill, she heard Ray was involved with another woman, and we both knew it wasn't me they were referring to. Surprisingly, I was not devastated when she told me this. Deep down inside I already knew because he did not contact me when his divorce had become final. Nonetheless, hearing about this other woman still hurt. I called Ray to confront him with what I had learned. Instead of fighting though, we had a nice conversation and he ended it with the promise to call me back soon.

Again months had passed without a word. Finally, on November 7, 1999 I accepted the fact he was not coming back into my life and I sent him the following note to bring closure to our relationship:

"I wish we could have tried for the "all" instead of the "nothing" because I miss not having you in my life. You will remain, however, in my heart and thoughts always." Sarah

The following Friday, he was back in my living room. There would no longer be secrets between us and over the next few weeks it became very clear where our relationship was headed. I finally got the answer to my long-awaited question "What if Ray and I were both single, would he finally choose me?" The answer – again — was no. Ray was in love with another woman and he married her instead.

Surrender

I N THE YEAR 2000 both Ray and Joe had remarried. This time, however, it was not difficult for me to say goodbye to either one. I was able to let them both go with love.

I continued to follow my desire to become an intuitive consultant which was proving to be more difficult than I thought. Building clientele at the store was a very slow process. Some days there would only be one or two people dropping in for a reading, sometimes no one at all. Fred, when advertising the store on the radio and in local newspapers was also promoting my business as well. One day, Kara, one of his radio advertising representatives, contacted me to see if I would do readings for a party the radio station was holding for their clientele on a cruise ship in exchange for free advertising. I agreed. This led for other promotions for me to do upcoming events at other local businesses. Gradually, I was meeting a lot of interesting people. I also found groups of like-minded people who practiced complimentary medicine such as acupuncture, kinesiology, and other modalities. In addition, I was also meeting wonderful people through church who shared a lot of the same beliefs I did.

Yet, meeting my financial obligations was becoming more difficult. Credit card debt was adding up very quickly and my monthly divorce settlement checks from Joe were going to come to an end within a few months. I also knew Fred was thinking about closing his store and moving to another location.

Eventually, it became apparent I would have to find other ways to supplement my income so I signed up with a temporary employment agency. Even though I did not want to go back to the corporate world, I gave in and started accepting long-term assignments, most of which were at a local hospital. Over a period of time, full-time positions had been offered to me, but I turned them down as I was adamant about working only part time so I could continue my spiritual work. Then, through the temporary agency, I was offered and accepted a part time position with a company that turned out to be owned by an old high school friend. However, I could not become their employee officially until my contract with the agency was up. Consequently, I was to work for them for a couple of months through the agency until they could hire me. Unfortunately, within a short time span, I realized the job was not a good fit for me and, since I dislike giving up on anything, I prayed to God for help in releasing me from the commitment I had made to the agency and to my friend. I received an answer to my prayer the same day when I returned home from work and the phone rang; it was the agency telling me that my friend had some unexpected financial changes and could not hire a part time employee at this time. Freed from my position, the next day the temporary agency had another long term assignment for me at a local hospital.

While working at the hospital I had made many friends, one in particular was with Grace. In her spare time she was a volunteer for a nonprofit organization. In 2003 their Board of Directors were looking for someone to manage their database and Grace had recommended me for the position. I accepted their offer of working out of my home approximately 10 hours a week for $500 a month. Then in July 2004 I applied for a part-time secretarial position at the hospital and was hired. Even though it appeared I was going backwards in my career, it met the criteria I was looking for in addition to providing me with unexpected medical and vacation benefits.

For a few years I was able to keep my head above water financially until 2009 when the credit card industry changed how they were doing business. My minimum payments, which I was just able to make, were going to double. Knowing there was no way I could make any more payments, I started contacting my creditors to see if they would work with me. All but one agreed, and without this one willing to work with me, I knew I would not be able to make my payments. Seeking spiritual guidance, I asked the angels for help. For it is when I listen to the angels I am able to find solace by writing letters to them asking for guidance, a practice one of my client's had shared with me – it's called automatic writing – you start off with the first line: Dear One, know that we love you and... So I started writing...

Dear One, know that we love you and all is well. You must learn to trust more – practice what you preach to others. Illusion versus reality – all is not what it appears to be. You will know soon enough what to do. You will have what you need – strength, courage and most of all love. Look within for what you want most, that is where it all begins – with you – then the rest will fall into place. Think positive thoughts. Patience my love, tomorrow will look brighter. All is well. It always has been. Stay focused and what you need to know will be revealed to you. Soon Sarah. Your life is about to change. Once again have faith – it is what you preach to others, practice what you preach. All is well. We are with you always. All our love, Angels of Light

What a difference a day makes! I had clarity on what I needed to do; I contacted a lawyer who advised me to file for bankruptcy. It was the solution to my problem, and it freed me to start anew.

A Fairy Tale Ending

⬦

WHEN THE ANNOUNCEMENT OF my bankruptcy hit the newspaper, Faith called to let me know she had seen it. Surprisingly, many people at work saw it too. Some people were judging me while others were asking if there was anything they could do to help. I, on the other hand, believed I was meant to go through this experience so I could help clients who came to me for advice on the subject.

Others would seek me out for advice on other matters as well. As time went on, throughout the hospital employees were discovering what I did for a living outside the office. Some had been customers at the "Store" and others had either heard about me through community education classes or from those who had come to me for readings. Gina, a hospital employee, sought me out for guidance regarding her love life. There were definitely parts of her story I could relate to.

Over thirty years had passed since Gina had moved away from

her high school sweetheart and first love. Within five years after moving, she had married another and later divorced. Years had gone by without a significant other in her life. She came to see me wondering if there would be someone in her future. A psychic she had gone to years before had described to her in detail the person who would be coming into her life. I too confirmed seeing this person.

Gina continued to think about her first love and how she always compared other men to him – no one ever made her feel the way he did. Then one day she bought a computer with internet and sometime later received an unexpected email from him. The communications continued and two months later she flew to her hometown to spend time with him. At first sight, they knew they would be spending the rest of their lives together. Upon her return to Chicago, Gina set the wheels in motion for a transfer within her company back to her hometown. In August, she was offered the transfer and moved back a month later. They got married shortly thereafter. Gina had her fairy tale ending. Would I?

Predestination

◄○►

I BELIEVE SOME THINGS IN life are predestined and that we have the capabilities of discovering what they are utilizing ancient tools. From numerology and Tarot, I learned how to intuitively explore life experiences, but after years of studying Astrology, I gained a better understanding as to **when** things might happen.

According to Astrology, the moment we are born we enter into an energy field vibration that will influence our strengths, weaknesses, opportunities and challenges in this lifetime. Hence, after years of study, I have come to believe a person's date of birth provides the key as to when they may be faced with life experiences.

For example, I was 30 years old when Joe and I got married. The tarot card represented by the number 30 is the Four of Wands, marriage being one of the inner meanings of this card. We married on the 30th of March which adds up to 33 (3+30 = 33), 33 being my Life Lesson Number. Years later my father would die on a 33 vibration day, May 28th (add 5 for May + 28 for the day = 33).

In addition to discovering some of my Life Lesson dates and events, I started paying attention to the things taking place in my life during my birth month as I believe this to be a key timeframe every year too. In numerology, June is associated with the number 6, and in Tarot, 6 is associated with the Lovers Card. Looking back over my journal, I was surprised to discover some of the things that happened during my birth month:

- June 1995, my life changed when I saw Ray again.
- June 1997, Ray sat in my living room reading the first draft of my manuscript.
- June 1998, Ray's divorce was final.
- June 2000, Ray married another

Another component I believe is key every month in discovering when I might be faced with potential opportunities and/or challenges is the day I was born. Thus, on the 10th of every month, I heighten my awareness as to the events taking place in my life, the people crossing my path, and how I feel. For example:

June 10th, days before Ray's marriage, I had turned 48. In tarot, the number 48 is associated with The Eight of Hearts, and here are just a few intuitive interpretations of this card:

Inner Strength regarding matters of the heart, Questioning one's relationship with another – is it over? Emotional, Loneliness, Abandonment issues, Moving in a new direction. Letting go.

June 10th, the year I turned 54, I received a gift from my friend Sophie, a DVD — The Secret by Rhonda Byrne. In Tarot, 54 is represented by the Princess of Swords. Intuitively, one of the interpretations of this card is hearing news from someone or "**secrets**" revealed.

The following year, August 10th, two months after I turned 55 (55 being my Destiny Number), my brother Lee passed away.

Over the years, I have learned to accept whatever is meant to be. Yet, there are some events that are harder to handle than others.

Timing Is Everything

<o>

I N June 2014, I was diagnosed with triple negative breast cancer. After meeting with several doctors, I followed their advice to have chemotherapy and radiation treatments. During that time, considering I might die sooner than later, I thought about my life and how my decisions and actions had affected others. Surprisingly, I was not afraid of the unknown, but I did have one regret about not pursuing my dream of becoming a writer. A couple of times I had submitted a manuscript to several publishers on my "timing is everything" concept only to be rejected. In 2012 my friend, Jennifer, had called to tell me about a contest Balboa Press, a division of Hay House was running for those wanting to become the next Hay House author. I entered and did not win. I then lost interest in writing.

In November 2015 the doctors had pronounced me cancer free, but it would take almost another year for me to build back up my stamina. In addition to my health limitations, other changes were taking place in my department at work that would require more adjusting on my part. Realizing that to be true, I decided to retire in October 2016 and focus on building my intuitive consultation business.

In **June** 2017 I opened an office in downtown Chicago and signed a year's lease. I also joined networking groups, attended meetings and social events. Several months later I discovered I didn't like working in an office anymore.

Little by little I was spending less time working and more time creating unproductive habits. This was brought to my attention while I was having a conversation with a motivational life coach at a networking event. He simply asked me what a normal week in my life looked like and I started listing off my daily routine:

- wake up and watch a movie for a couple of hours while enjoying my morning coffee.
- get up, have breakfast, shower, dress
- get ready to go running with my sister, mother; shopping, drinks with friends and – OH – maybe see a client or two during the week.

  This is when it hit me that I had to decide if I wanted to be retired or build my business.

The very next morning I started my new routine:

May 7, 2018

o   Meditate, asking for guidance as to what I should be doing

o   Watch motivational and religious speakers on You Tube

o   Exercise

May 8, 2018, one day later after meditating and seeking guidance, my dream of becoming a writer resurfaced when from out of the blue I get an email from a Balboa Press Agent, six years later after having entered one of their contests:

"Sarah, I tried contacting you earlier regarding the opportunity of becoming the next Hay House author from Balboa Press. Unfortunately, I have been unable to reach you using the phone number I have on file..."

I emailed her back and signed a contract with Balboa Press that day.

Dreams Do Come True

◄o►

OVER THE NEXT FEW months, I focused on my book and attended more networking events. Soon, realizing I didn't like attending meetings, I came up with my own idea for a networking group for women only. My intent was to host this event monthly along with another business female friend. I didn't have to look far.

Paige, my insurance agent, had come over to have me sign some papers, and I asked her if she would come to my mix and mingle. Being a member of a country club, she asked me if I would like to hold my event there and I said "Sure." Then she asked me if it would be okay if she and her husband provided the wine and I said "Absolutely!" From there she created a Facebook page for me, posted the event, and took care of the reservations. It was a great success, and we have been co-hosting this event every month since then.

In addition to establishing a networking group, another

opportunity arose in January to promote my business. My friend Haley, a board member of our church, called to see if I would be interested in doing an intuition class there some Sunday in addition to being a guest speaker. I committed to doing both in March 2019.

As the time drew closer to giving my talk, I wondered what I was going to say that would be of interest to others. Several ideas came to mind but I decided to meditate for clarity as to what my message would be. The next day I started writing my outline for my topic: Dreams – Real or Imagined.

Throughout my life my dreams have brought me messages of things to come. In my teens I had what I called my "weather forecast dreams: I dreamt of tornados, hurricanes, flooding, and fire. Over time I actually came to like these dreams because I was able to intuit their hidden meanings as to what was coming. The wind and water dreams revealed emotional changes in relationships while fire usually represented a physical move in career or home. Sometimes, to validate my intuitive interpretations of my dreams and to learn more about my future, I would seek additional guidance from Crystal, a local psychic.

At age 25, after having dreamt of a major fire, I went to see "The Reverend," a very intuitive man and the founder of the church where I was going to be a guest speaker. He too saw a major change in my life, and it was later that year I moved to San Diego, CA.

While living in San Diego I started experiencing lucid dreaming in which I knew I was in a dream state to where I could direct my story line in any direction I chose. These dreams I paid very close attention to detail such as colors, did I turned right or left, how did I feel – was I happy, sad or afraid. This type of dreaming I loved because, being the director of my dreams, they all had happy endings and I always ended up the heroine.

Then there were those dreams I prayed for to come true. I prayed for love, marriage, a home and security. In 1983 all these dreams came true and for twelve years I was very happy – then I wasn't. Something was missing in my life, and I sought to find the answer by seeking guidance from Angel, a San Diego psychic. She stressed that I needed to go deeper into my subconscious by meditating and developing my sixth sense. By heeding her advice I discovered how I could be of service to others as an intuitive consultant. In turn, others offered their services to help me too.

Jill, a referral from my friend Lynn, came to see me in July 2016 for a consultation. Instantly, we bonded and shared our hopes and wishes for the future. When I told her one of my desires was to create my own oracle cards, she offered to help me as she was a graphic designer. In March 2017, my cards became a reality and we had 200 decks printed.

Sharing my desire to become a writer with others also generated offers of help. As I drew closer to completing my manuscript, I sought out advice from my friend Kay who had experience editing stories for a publishing company.

Kay and I met in 1996; she was one of my first clients at Fred and Gail's metaphysical store. Since that time we have kept in touch. In October 2018 I received an email from her letting me know she and her husband, Gary were moving to Tahiti and I was invited to their going away party. The week before they left Kay stopped by to drop off a gift for me. As we chatted, I shared with her my dream of wanting to become an author. It was then I discovered she was a volunteer judge for a publishing company whenever they ran contests for aspiring authors. Kay would review some of the entries and help to select finalists for the publisher's final decision. When I told her about my book and contract with Balboa Press, she offered her services to help edit it. It was an offer I could not refuse.

In February 2019 I sent Kay several chapters to review. She was very encouraging in that she liked what she had read so far. Over the next several weeks I continued to send her more chapters. The more she read, the more excited she was to see how my story was going to end. I too was wondering the same thing until a month later then I knew.

In March 2019, standing before the church congregation, I concluded my talk on dreams with advice I had received from my angel oracle cards to encourage everyone to dream big and be bold enough to live their dream.

This message inspired and motivated me to finish my book with Kay's help — in Tahiti. A month later I was on a flight to her place to fulfill my dream. For two glorious weeks she and her husband spoiled me rotten. In the mornings I would work a little bit on my manuscript, but the majority of the time was spent sightseeing and eating out at fabulous restaurants. Kay and Gary were the perfect hosts, and I enjoyed my stay with them very much.

Returning home to my business and family obligations, I found it necessary to schedule times to work on my manuscript. Five months later, on September 12, 2019, a 33 vibration day and my Life Lesson Number (9+ 12 + 2+0+1+9 = 33), I submitted my manuscript to Balboa Press. I fulfilled my dream of finishing my story knowing it would lead to more questions and more dreams – real or imagined: Would I become a successful writer; would I fall in love again and live a life dedicated to helping others? I hope so.

Then I remembered the last message I had received years ago at the vortex in Sedona when the angels had whispered "believe," and I believe in happy endings.

Fortunately, I also believe in a Higher Power and I trust that whatever is meant to be, will be.

S INCE 1996 SARAH HAS been providing Intuitive/Spiritual
guidance to others utilizing Astrology, Numerology and other
intuitive tools. Her mission in life is to help others expand their
own inner awareness and to validate what they already know to
be true